Happy [illegible]
to you !!

love,
Des

1990.

Show Us The Moon

THE DUBLIN DAYS OF

Lar Redmond

BRANDON

Brandon Book Publishers Ltd
Dingle, Co Kerry, Ireland
and 27 South Main Street
Wolfeboro, New Hampshire 03894-2069, USA

British Library Cataloguing in Publication Data
Redmond, Lar
Show us the moon.
1. Dublin. Social life, 1920-1940.
Personal Observations
I. Title
941.8'.350822'0924

ISBN 0-86322-098-3

Cover design: Brendan Foreman
Typeset by Koinonia Ltd, Manchester
Printed by Richard Clay Ltd, Bungay, Suffolk

Contents

1
CHILDHOOD DAYS

The Aroma Of Sunday Mornings

Put me anywhere, blindfolded, in the Liberties of my boyhood, and I could tell where I was by the smell; I could nearly tell the time as well. Odours, pongs, whiffs and stinks marked your passage through this area. The cloying smell of hops and grain spelled James's Gate; New Street was the smell of an ill-tended public lavvo mixed with the lime works, and the stench of tenement houses. Donnelly's bacon factory, reeking of burning hair and steam said "Cork Street". But the king of all the smells, known as "a funk", came from O'Keefe's the knackers in the same street. It was endured cheerfully enough for O'Keefe's was the source of bait and carried memories of perch, canals and fishing with it.

We fished with the larvae of the bluebottle, "chandlers" to us, though Izaac Walton called them "gentles" but then he never got his in Cork Street. There was nothing gentle about that area then. You risked a "lurrying up" every time. Fraught with danger the chandlers were doubly precious when the fish were biting, and you could skin a chandlerless boy and bankrupt him in the comic cut or cigarette card department for half a dozen.

The very brickwork of the streets reeked of pigs' cheeks and cabbage. Mix all the smells together, stand on the top of Christ Church Hill with the wind in the right quarter, and you had the distilled essence of the Liberties. It was the scent of ambition never fulfilled, of youth, and love and sadness, and joy; it was the sweet smell of home.

But of all the bouquets ever created by God the sweetest of all was the aroma of the Liberties on Sunday morning when the one fry-up of the week hit the pan.

Unfortunately, it was also Communion morning, and in those too severe days not even a drop of water was allowed. All the way up Dolphin's Barn the sizzling pans sent out waves of seduction as animals, masquerading as people, prepared for a heathen orgy, while your tormented stomach turned over. Already hungry an hour, a boy had sinned many times in his mind before Mass, with constant prayer the only protection. Striving to fix the mind on heaven and the next world, with paradise on the pan in this one! When the spirit should have been thrilled with holy joy it was attacked by the foul flesh, corruputed by thoughts of sinking the fangs into Hafner pork products, their elite corps of black and white puddings and peerless sausages. Never since then have sausages been made so succulent or so sinful. Kneeling in the chapel with drooling chops, anticipating the joy of the first sausage hitting the empty sack, digestive juices flooding out. . .

"Oh, dear Lord, forgive me for my wicked thoughts but I'm only a little hungry boy an' we only get the one fry a week" . . .

"Tryin' teh get around yer Creator," snarls conscience, "Yeh devious little Dublin gurrier." And then, loaded with the fresh sin of hypocrisy, I prayed for forgiveness, face set in a mould of piety, stomach rumbling for sausages.

And so, a Homeric struggle through the Mass, inching towards the door towards the end, and then bursting out, running down the Barn, the street still full of the magic of rashers and eggs and Hafners, with good, hardworking people, enjoying a late breakfast, as I would soon be enjoying mine.

Man, dear, the likes of that Sunday morning breakfast will never come again. It is only a memory now, along with the firm that made pork products to a recipe stolen from Fairyland. I grow old among a race who have never even smelt the real McCoy, much less eaten it, a debased wheat-flake generation, who haunt the super-marts, God bless the mark. I should pity them, I know, but I don't. They're too well up and they think they know it all.

The Long War

I was tired looking at the Custom House burning, bored with the non-stop display of flames and sparks that I could see from our neighbour's window, and sleepy, so Mam put me to bed in our gloomy back room.

In the morning I would wake up, Mam beside me, and she would give me a snuggle. My elder brother was rarely around, having stolen the heart of the childless woman in the front room, and likely to sleep there, and I would have Mam all to myself. On the morning I was never to forget, I woke up and nudged her. She turned, kissed me briefly, said "Good morning child". . . and that was that!

Shocked, I lay there listening to her soft laughter and the deeper note of a man's voice. It was my father's, I was to learn, and he was on the run, risking his life to spend a night with his love. But he had stolen my love. She had no time for me now, gay and alight as I had never seen her, a butterfly I did not recognize.

Presently she arose and started to cook breakfast, with this man in trousers and singlet standing behind her, calling her "Dolly", arms around her, and she laughing and loving every minute of it. Absentmindedly she gave me breakfast in bed and I sullenly ate it, while those two sat at the table, smiling and talking all the time. I hated the man and wished he would go away. And my ill-will had not long to wait. The soft, staccato knock I had come to know sounded on our door and a young Shinner came in.

"Get dressed quick," he told my father, "Yer man

downstairs has been to the coppers."

Always the man downstairs was to be feared, a drunken old informer who'd do anything for whiskey and who died that night, full of booze and bullets. In a flash they had gone and my familiar white-faced mother was back, trembling, clearing all signs of breakfast away, while I watched the two disappear over the back wall.

The soldiers came, as expected, and went and then, from the direction of Talbot Street, came the sound of heavy gunfire. Mam nearly lost her mind. Even I had never seen her so bad, but her hysteria was wasted. Dad was unarmed and had plodded through the cordon by leading a bread van horse. His friend Paddy, however, was armed and had plenty of bullets. The Shinners were getting the upper hand and, young and reckless, he decided to shoot it out, and did. . . taking three Tans with him.

In the afternoon of this terrible day another hysterical woman came to us, carrying a three day old baby. It was her Paddy who had died. Two half-mad women, crying together, one with sorrow, the other with both sorrow and relief. Finally, as darkness came, the woman went away, leaving our room in blessed peace.

But that night my mother's nerve finally broke. At about eleven o'clock I was hauled out of bed, bundled in a blanket and rushed down the echoing stairs as we ran for it. All around us was the roar of heavy gunfire as the Shinners took toll for that morning's killing, having ambushed a couple of truck-loads of troops. Through this mayhem my crazed mother ran, shoving the pram through piles of broken glass. . . shots. . . shouts. . . "Take cover. . . yeh crazy bitch. . ."

Once over O'Connell Bridge the worst of the battle was behind us, but my mother never slackened her gasping run until we stood on the top of Cork Hill. There before me was the Liberties, where I would live for the next fourteen years, the crucible that would mould me, shape me, make me or break me.

Presently Mam located me in the pram, half suffocated.
"Are yawl right?" she asked.
"Yes, Dolly," I said stoutly.
"Dolly, is it?" she said to herself, and gave a little laugh.
And it came to me then that she was not very old, she was very pretty really. . . lovely, especially when she smiled. Strangely, she never afterwards looked old to me, not even when she was growing old. Soon after our perilous dash through the streets the Truce was declared: the War of Independence was over.

But a new war, one that would last far longer, started that day. It was between my father and me. We seemed always opposed to each other; we rubbed each other up the wrong way and my mother, loving us both, was often torn apart. He tried and I tried to bridge the gulf, but it was no good. Nothing worked for long, and I never knew why.

Until one day in an Australian desert in a fit of bitter homesickness I remembered the morning of the man in the bed and in a blue flash realized the truth. Like many other vendettas it was founded in the love of a woman, and that woman was his wife and my mother.

When I was no longer young and he was very old I told him, for towards the end we were great pals. He laughed softly, a little mistily, for she was long gone. The thing that had kept us apart for a lifetime now bonded us together, the one love. He has gone now, too, but wherever he is his Dolly is not far away, and things have been put in their proper order. I was but a token of their love for each other and can no longer come between them. So be it. I am content.

An Ill Wind

In what Hollywood describes as "The Roaring Twenties", things were tough, as never before, in the Liberties. Its industries were dying. The one poplin factory left was on its last legs, the silk trade was dead, and almost all the tanneries were closed. The war between motor-car and horse was grimly fought out in the narrow streets; in the personal conflict between the drivers we were treated to many a delightful scrap when the trucks refused to give right of way. Adding to the growing number of unemployed the forges were giving up the ghost; the harness makers stood at the street corners, living fossils in their own lifetime.

It was worse, if one went by the papers, across the Irish Sea. Scottish miners, dressed in the proud regalia of the clans, played the pipes through the shabby Liberties streets for money. Hard hit themselves, the people gave generously, for these men were on strike, locked in combat with the coal barons, and their families were starving. Wild men, playing wild Celtic music, to the wild Celts who had stormed the Pale and taken it, at last.

Great Britain was a shambles. That land fit for heroes to live in had turned out no better for the working class than the new state across the water, but Irishmen, like Dad, had freedom. . . all the freedom in the world to starve; though I don't think that is exactly what he had in mind when he took on "The h-Empire".

But some things were happening, too. The national flag (pronounced "the Trickiller" by British aristocrats) flew proudly over the GPO. The old tongue, almost extinct, became the official language of the state, and an

Irishman, Colonel Fitzmaurice, had flown the Atlantic with two Germans. Some Dail Deputies raised a laugh by laying bunches of rhubarb, carrots and cauliflowers at Queen Victoria's statue on Leinster Lawn, jolly little offerings that would have been swiped in two seconds had her statue been in the Liberties, and with custard and a bit of scrag end of beef made up a stew for some pale-faced little gurriers living on bread and cocoa. . . Shell Cocoa, the cheapest.

In my own family the standard of living declined while our numbers increased. Jobs for carpenters were scarce but if there was one going anywhere, even as far out as Stillorgan, Dad got it and cycled there, hail, rain or snow. He was a battler, and the guts he showed against the Tans he took to civvy street, while many of his compatriots existed on the dole and on their memories, lost without a gun.

When the Wall Street crash came it scarcely caused a ripple in the Coombe. It was reported in the papers that pedestrians walked close to the skyscrapers, a precaution against bankrupts hurling themselves from upper storeys, but nobody in the Liberties ever ran such a risk. It was hard enough to live, without committing suicide! It was the same, only better, when the Economic War started. The Irish Free State stopped paying for land they owned anyway, and Britain replied by closing the ports to Irish cattle. All over the country cattle were slaughtered for their hides and the carcasses were thrown in ditches. The Free State was brought to its knees and from that position, which the Irish were used to, fought on. The hardship inflicted on the farmers was appalling, but in the Liberties the sun was shining. My father deplored the terrible state of the country, but we were better fed than ever before. For us little gurriers, tucking into big steaks or hacking away at Sunday's roast, God was in His heaven and the world was all right.

As they say, "It's an ill wind that blows nobody good".

Cockpits Of The Mind

At the back of my grandfather's house in Clanbrassil Street there was a scrap-yard that seemed to have been there since the beginning of time. All the flotsam and jetsam of the Victorian era had been gathered here. Old-fashioned bathtubs jutted out of piles of timber salvaged from gutted Georgian houses, for the destruction of Dublin had already begun. Everything from a commode to a copper cylinder could be bought here and it was the Mecca of jobbing carpenters and plumbers seeking cheap lead and timber. It all seemed ancient to me and I took little interest in the piled-up debris until I went to see a movie that was taking the world by storm.

I saw it at the age of eleven years and I saw it again at fifty and it still remains, to me, the greatest anti-war film ever made. *All Quiet On the Western Front* brought the filth, stench and terror of warfare into the cinema. The Royal, where I saw it with my father, was suddenly filled with screaming shells and shrapnel, and I cowered before a blizzard of bullets in a shell hole with the young German boys on screen. It had only taken the twentieth century fourteen years to show its paces. The industrial revolution had come to the battlefield and cavalry regiments withered and died in the mud. The ponderous tank advanced over all. Even the sky held terror, for snarling planes were aloft, flying low over the cowering soldiers, mowing them down. My interest in the scrap-yard grew rapidly after that horrendous movie, for right below the Grandad's window were wings and fusilages of World War I planes, which on closer inspection revealed bullet holes in their canvas covering, scars of actual combat. It was one of these that had killed Katinsky, the young hero's comrade in *All Quiet. . .* My imagination soared.

But it was not until another war movie came to the screen, called *Hells Angels,* that I really came into my own. This picture, although not without some merit, showed a more glamorous conflict, far above the crawling rats in the mud below. Here the handsome gladiators of the twentieth century battled it out in the sky over Flanders, young eagles, some of whom would shortly fall out of the blue with flaming plumage.

The next time I was in the Grandad's, as always his cronies were there, and inevitably the talk turned to the late Great War. The Grandad's eldest son had fought all through it, even the lemming-like landing at Gallipoli, and like Katty Barry, the man who fought the monkey on the Naas Road, was demobbed without a scratch, at nineteen. He had joined up at fourteen years of age!

"The Dublin Fusiliers were the boys for Jerry," my Grandad would say, "Jerry doesn't like cold steel. . ."

The Dubs, it seemed, loved it, though that is not the way it came across to me from the German movie. But in jig time the pleasant room, with one whole wall covered with singing canaries, would be full of the reek of cordite, the deadly chatter of machine guns, and the gallant Dubs, bayonets flashing, would charge and Flight Commander Lar Redmond would coolly step from the back room into the cockpit below in the scrap-yard and roar off.

Von Richtofen and his circus were strafing the airfield while I was twisting desperately to gain height, barely missing Blackpits School and Fitzpatrick's pub; the Baron, in his red plane close behind as I found shelter in a cloud, and then. . . blue sky and below me the enemy at my mercy. Swinging my plane into a screaming dive, pouring lead into the German's plane. . . the dying Baron giving me a gallant salute before nose-diving into the Lousy Acre, Patrick's Park. Smiling crookedly, I saluted a noble enemy. . .

"Dashed bad luck, old chap," I murmured softly, and. . .

"What's that?" said the Grandad.

I lied and told him I had said nothing.

"Well," he said, turning to his pals, "me son Jack was leadin' the Dubs across No Man's Land when. . ."

It all seems so puny now, almost parochial, yet six million soldiers perished in that old war, and twice as many more in the dreadful flu that came from the stinking Flanders mud. Enough for a thousand years, one would think. Yet us kids of that time were born with a truer insight than our fathers or the politicians of the day. We knew through the pores of our skin that it was only half time, that a resumption of hostilities was inevitable. We did not know of gas chambers and concentration camps. We had never heard of Hiroshima or Nagasaki which, when reduced to radioactive rubble, would cast the longest shadow over mankind ever. Today's kids know that, though. They do not play the silly game I played from bullet-riddled cockpits of the mind.

They sniff their glue, steal their cars, get stoned on drugs in the shadow of Armageddon. Through the pores of their skin they, too, were born with the knowledge that we are all in the front line now. This is their inheritance. And yet old fogies wag their heads wisely, gravely tut-tut and wonder what is wrong with the young people of today. What indeed! That is some inheritance we have given them.

Female Of The Species

When I was only a boy the Dublin Whiskey Distillery in Bridgefoot Street closed down for ever, adding more to the long list of Liberties industries that had already gone to the wall. O'Keefe's the knackers at the bottom of Cork Street was bought by a foreign company who merely sabotaged its capacity to make glue and, having smashed the equipment, resold it. I once worked with a man who told me all about the affair, he having got a few weeks' work cutting up four-inch pipes of half-inch thick copper, irreplaceable. He told me the glue made here was world famous and was even bought in China and Japan. There was only one company still manufacturing poplin left and the silk weaving had passed with the Huguenots into history. The tanneries that had once polluted the Poddle died one by one and Henry Ford was finishing off the harness-makers by wiping out the horse. With its demise went the forge; the blacksmith, that man of "large and sinewy hands", stood on the street corner with the same hands in empty pockets.

The poverty was appalling in the twenties and thirties and I have never, thank God, had to witness its like again, except, of course, in Third World countries. But in my schooldays we had a Third World from the top of Dolphin's Barn to Christ Church and Winetavern Street. There the Liffey halted it, and what happened on the north, uncharted side of Dublin, where rumour said they ate their young, was good enough for them! Over there was the other side of the moon.

So, with the Liberties men jobless, it fell to the lioness of the pride to provide for the large brood that was the average family of those days. The dealers, the street trading women, were numbered in hundreds and fought the City Fathers grimly for possession of the pavements. With the passing of the British, the Irish government set out at once to clean up the capital. The first casualty of this onslaught was Monto, the "red light" district around Gardiner Street. The second were the dealers who, year by year, were squeezed out of the city centre. George's Street, Wexford Street and Camden Street put up the fiercest resistence, with empty tables and fireless rooms the spur. In the Liberties, as in Moore Street, these formidable ladies were never conquered and to this day continue to trade off the pavements. Pitches were jealously guarded and belonged to the trading elite, and that left thousands of women to look elsewhere.

A portion of them poured through Dolphin's Barn in autumn and springtime, in hail, rain or snow: cabbage planters and turnip snaggers bound for the market garden area around Sundrive Road and beyond. For this backbreaking labour they were paid a few coppers per hundred cabbages planted, and so badly needed was the money that they would work through a downpour until stopped by the overseer. It was no consideration for the women that made him call a halt, for cabbage had to be planted under proper conditions, and it hadn't learned to swim.

They went out in the morning like a cheerful gaggle of geese, and only too often trailed miserably home at night, soaked, cold and hungry. The indestructable women of the Pale, who lost the roses on their cheeks and paled only too soon. Glasnevin and Mount Jerome cemeteries were full of them.

Another occupation that reared many a family and sent many a woman to an early grave was scrubbing floors. The world was full of floors to be scrubbed, and scrubbed they were by Dublin's poor. "Do you want yer oul' lobby washed down" was no cheerful song then. The lobby was the landing at the top of a flight of stairs, and on their knees they scrubbed their ways to their personal Calvaries.

Still another job that uneducated women could do was taking in washing. "L.A.N.D.R.Y. took in", read a notice in a shop window, and some unfortunate woman worked bent over a corrugated washboard and steaming tin bath to make an honest shilling. The fortunate ones of this trade had jobs in Dublin's numerous laundries. Up a lane just off Barn Street was the Mirror Laundry where my pal's mother and two sisters worked. I had often remarked to myself their appearance of impeccable cleanliness. The reason was explained when Tom told me where they worked and that their one perk was their laundry could go through free. Tom's clothes, therefore, although shabby, were always clean and pressed, but beyond that his sisters and especially his mother, with her silver hair, had a positively bleached look. This was explained to me one hot summer's day when I passed the laundry to get buttermilk from Joyce's farm.

The windows of the one-storey laundry had been thrown open against the heat and steam was pouring out. I saw Tom's mother through the fog, hand-pressing some very expensive linen shirts. She was right beside the window and nodded to me. Further back I spotted the two sisters and grinned at them. They smiled through the steam and bent again to their work; sweet Nan of the porcelain beauty, who would be dead of tuberculosis in two years, waved to me. And I knew then, in a flash, the reason for their bleached appearance. They were virtually steam-cleaned, inside and out, Nan destroyed by overwork and lack of fresh air.

Let no one talk to me too much about the good old days! I remember them too clearly, and they were good only because I was young.

Christmas Morning In The Liberties

Christmas is coming, the goose is getting fat,
Please put a penny in the old man's hat

we sang as children, but even then the American turkey was starting to rival the goose in popularity, and in my early childhood my mother would ponder as to whether to get a turkey or a goose. Not for long, however. Very soon the Yankee gobbler gobbled up the Irish goose, and the old nursery rhyme lost some of its relevance if not its appeal.

The bit about putting a penny in the old man's hat, however, remained only too true, for Dublin's poverty, measured against today's standards, was appalling. Living on the edge of the Liberties, I had plenty of time to observe it at close quarters. My observation was unconscious and, being part of the place, I accepted what was around me but, as I grew older, not without question. There were compensations, though. There was a great sense of belonging to a close-knit community that I have never found in suburbia. Wages were low, and even those households that enjoyed constant employment had to struggle to make ends meet. We were all in the same boat, and hearts were more kindly then.

One of the things that bonded the women of our little community together was the "Didley Club". It was run by the most enterprising member among them, and well I remember taking the week's contribution to the organizer. Every thrifty wife and mother belonged to the Club, which started at the end of July, their savings being withdrawn at Christmas. This went a long way towards the extra cost of Yuletide which, in our large family, was considerable.

I well remember my mother's nail-biting experience of the week before the big day, when she would anxiously scan the shops, undecided whether to buy now or take a chance and hope the price of turkeys would drop. It seldom did, except in Moore Street, and then only late on Christmas Eve. On that day my mother would leave the house after tea to go "foraging", as she called it, and she would always came back, face aglow, triumphant, having once again gambled and won.

Already she would have all our toys lined up, hidden in some childless neighbour's house, and it was Dad's job to collect them and do Santa Claus. Once over the age of ten my gift was always roller skates, which I wore out by summer. But on Christmas morning summer was a million miles away, it was the springtime of my life; God had given me a singing voice as clear as a skylark and I warbled with the best in Clarendon Street choir, to which I and my younger brother belonged.

Christmas remains in my mind as always fine and mild, with a starry sky overhead, me telling my brother as we went along that the glittering north star was the one that guided the Three Wise Kings to the stable where Jesus slept. Mam saw us to the door and let us go without a qualm, even though we had to traverse some of the worst slums in Europe. Had violence been prevalent, these unfortunates who wasted away in tenement houses, jobless, living on bread and tea, could have easily been excused for resorting to it, but it was not so. There was little violence and women and children walked secure in that knowledge. All the way from Dolphin's Barn, past the tottering, high-gabled houses of the long departed Huguenots, through Ardee Street and the festering Coombe, past Patrick's Park and through Golden Lane, where gold was never seen. All our way lay through slums where entire families lived in one room and babies were born into a world of swaddling clothes, akin to the baby that had been born in a stable at Bethlehem. And from every window a tall red candle, given by the grocer to his customers, gleamed from behind flimsy curtains to guide the Three Kings to where the King of all Kings had been born.

And then it was across George's Street, under a sky full of stars that gleamed like diamonds, barely in time for seven o'clock Mass. A full choir, tenors and bass standing at the back, us boys, sopranos and altos, sitting in front; the hymns floating over the assembled throng; the joy of singing, of being young, never to grow old, to come here always on Christmas morning and sing the praises of the baby Jesus.

The memory of those times even now spreads over me like a benediction and is treasured. Other little boys all over Ireland, born into a better world, will set out again each Christmas morning to send their young voices heavenwards. Gentlemen songsters out on a spree! But their memories of Christmas will be no better than mine.

One For The Mots

In the Liberties of long ago the pageant of the seasons was not marked by falling leaves or blossoming flowers; it was the street games that told the story. Except, of course, for the annual sortie into the countryside for blackberries. There was a lot of secrecy among the big fellas about this for they always referred to the place that provided loads of "blackers" as "The Nack". Time after time they sloped off, always to come back loaded, but as the years slipped by we became the older ones and in our turn tried to preserve the secret of nature's storehouse of blackberries that we had located by trailing the others. It was in deep, deep countryside in Landsdowne Valley beside the Halfway House.

Chestnuts came after the blackers and found their way into the narrow streets. Conker was pitted against conker. Threaded on string, you could take on the others with them, and as you broke your opponents' chestnuts you became conqueror until someone broke you. One evening I was presented by my father with the largest, shiniest chestnut I had ever seen. He carefully bored a hole in it, threaded it on strong cord, and the following morning I sallied forth to cause devastation among my companions. Chestnut after chestnut broke before the assault of my monstrous champion and I was the proud conqueror of eleven when Nipper Fitz confronted me with a wizened pygmy of a thing and challenged me.

Grinning, I confidently took him on, blow after blow

being exchanged until, aghast, I watched my champion split and break on the next belt from the runt. I dissolved in tears and Nipper, grinning, was the conqueror of twelve. From that bitter experience I learned that if you wanted a champion of champions you had to season it for a whole year up the chimney. So I dried my tears, vowed vengeance, and stacked a dozen up the flue for next year. Alas, the following year when I collected them, bent on mayhem, I found I had neglected to hole them for string, and I broke every one trying to do so.

Hard on the heels of conkers came marbles, and here again I came a cropper. The same Nipper demolished a huge chalk marble I had paid a whole penny for with a speckled stone runt and left me in tears again. But I was learning. Soon I would be another "Nipper", putting manners on cheeky chisellers who got too big for their boots.

Christmas brought roller skates, scooters, and airguns, so that the next spate of street games came around Easter. It was then that tops became all the rage and you could lash away for hours with your cord whip, the trick being to make your top jump without capsizing and rolling sideways into the gutter. Around about this time the girls bought chalk and marked the pavement out in lines of latitude about three feet apart. Between lines was called a "bed". With a shoe polish tin filled with clay, the game started, the idea being that standing on one leg you had to toe the tin, called a "pikky", from one bed to another. If the pikky landed on a line you were out. If not correctly placed, you hopped onto a line, and that also was out. Other girls preferred playing shop, so that every corner was filled with bargaining customers and shopkeepers, who used small pieces of broken china for money.

We never felt the need for a recreation ground. The Square was big enough for football and private enough for a game of pontoon, which was played with a dog-eared deck for cigarette cards. And then, summer holidays coming on, there were the quarries for fishing, the canal for swimming, and over the Barn Bridge the fragrant fields went all the way to Cork. The girls and the flowers appeared then in force; like goldfinches and linnets, colourful and gay, in their printed cotton frocks the girls filled the Square with their chatter and song.

Hand in hand they faced each other in long lines, dancing backwards and forwards, and any unwary lad passing through would quickly find himself trapped, as I was one blessed day long ago. They joined hands behind me and then in front, forming a pretty circle and, dancing around me, sang,

Phyllis Dowling ses she'll die,
If she doesn't get the fella wit' the marble eye.

And they pushed poor Phyllis forward to where I stood scarlet-faced.

"Go on Phyllis, yeh know yeh love him," they shouted.

And I got a soft, hurried kiss, which I returned amid roars and cheers, all the married women wistfully watching, laughing on the edge of tears, calling to my mother, "Ye'll have teh watch that Lar. . . That fella 'ill be wan for the mots." The whole place full of joy on that God-given day that I would remember down the maze of the years. Innocence! The cries that followed me as I broke free and ran for it. One thing was certain, then and always. I was one for the mots. And what was wrong with that? For what little Dubliner could possibly get anything better in life than a little Liberties mot?

A Good Feed

Across the Liffey where, according to Liberties lore, the city turns cannibal and begins to eat its young, lies the haymarket, Smithfield, geographically only a few hundred yards away yet light years from the teeming alleys of Dean Swift. Nevertheless, it was an integral part of my native place.

Through Dolphin's Barn Street came the produce of half Leinster, and in the autumn came the hay-bogeys, low-wheeled flat carts piled high with the plunder of many a meadow, rumbling over the cobbles, filling the mean streets with fragrance and killing the reek of poverty for a time. It was fair play, then, to attack the hills of hay and give the milkman's horse a good feed. This was the time when any boy like me who possessed a dog laid by a supply of warm bedding against the cold of a place like the outside lavatory where Nigger, my bitch, slept. It wasn't really stealing, I claimed, for, like Robin Hood, I was only robbing the rich to succour the poor.

On autumn mornings, when the streets were full of the smell of horses and hay, I mitched from school and, with Nigger, followed the tide of hay, ending up in Smithfield. Here I spent many a day in heaven. The huge square would be filled with golden mounds, and in the middle all sight and sound of the surrounding squalid area was lost. This was when I became Finn McCool, my crossbred collie became Scolín, and we hunted the Irish Elk without mercy. On these occasions I spoke only Gaelic, but Nigger, like many another little Liberties product, had a built-in resistance to her native tongue and wilfully refused to understand. When I said "Stad" she ran, when instructed to "Tar anseo" she went. Always I had to end the game, defeated, and go to Canada where I became a Mountie, dogging a fugitive from justice. While Nigger, my last husky, snarled the wolves away I would be climbing a golden snow drift, five hundred miles from Fort McKenzie, in the heart of Dublin.

I loved that dog as only a boy can love his first. When I was in disgrace she knew and would console me with an understanding lick and race around me, barking, in the green fields of Crumlin, making me forget that the whole world was against me. For her I became a real thief and robbed the sack of dog biscuits in the Blanchardstown Mill shop, until my shortsighted heart-throb Marion noticed and placed it beyond reach. But by that time Nigger had a shining black coat, a wet nose, and sparkling eyes. My conscience never troubled me, for the decision to rob had been forced on me.

Nigger was a coward, and anything on four legs that could stand up and bark could run her, and all my urging achieved nothing. Tail between legs, she always ran off, shaming me. One day on the towpath of the canal a small tyke half her size attacked, and Nigger jumped straight into the water. A quiet, doggy, country man standing nearby told me that "that dog needs a good feed". He was looking at my well-worn gansey and scuffed plimsolls, and my face flamed as I read his mind.

"Mister," I told him, "that dog is fed twice a day."

"On what?" asked the doggy man.

"On bread and very sweet tea," I answered.

"That's no good for a dog," I was told. "Her coat is dull, her eyes are dull, everything about her is dull. What she needs is buildin' up with dog biscuits."

So then and there I made my decision: built up with dog biscuits she would be.

Later I often walked the towpath and wished that the quiet man would come along, and one day he did, accompanied by a huge Alsatian bitch which was snarling and spoiling for a fight. She came straight for Nigger, obviously intending to eat her for lunch, and I nearly got sick with fear. But Nigger, snarling, stood her ground and sank her teeth into the Alsatian's throat. Howling with terror, the Alsatian ran off, dragging Nigger with her, for she was twice the size. Eventually Nigger came back, barking her victory, alive as never before. The quiet country man was stunned; he asked me if it was the same dog, and had I been giving her monkey glands?

"Dog biscuits," I answered proudly, "morning, noon and

night."

"Begob," he said softly, "'tis marvellous what a good feed will do for a city mongrel!"

I could have told him that there was many another, where I came from, who could have been similarly transformed if taken off a diet of bread and tea; that there were too many who were being liberated from the Liberties forever, crossing the Jordan via Mount Jerome for the want of a good feed. But, of course, I was too young then to figure that one out. And so, instead, with my heart pounding with joy, I strutted off down life's potholed towpath, with never a cloud in the sky.

2
Liberties Ways

Show Us The Moon

A lot of nostalgic nonsense has been written in recent years about the Liberties, but the Liberties of my boyhood was a place of stark want where the evil spirit of the Gorta* stalked every street. The merciless Gorta, he who had slain this nation, rattled the doors of houses in the Coombe and Pimlico. An old, congested, filthy and poverty-stricken place, great tradesmen went out from here to build the grand Georgian squares of Dublin while their own ancient part of the city was falling apart at the seams, a teeming rabbit warren, a down-at-heel Irish kasbah on the Poddle. Nobody ever spent a childhood here and escaped without being branded. You could adopt a new way of speaking, even a new country, but the thinking remained Liberties thinking, and you were still Dublin to the core.

Striding through the concrete canyons of New York muffled up against the piercing cold, or shuffling through the red talcum dust and stinking heat that is an Australian desert, this place, if it owned you, could come at you with shattering impact and while you were finding your way along, hating the lunar landscape, you would suddenly be elsewhere, and to save your sanity would run down Meath Street or Francis Street to buy a Jew's harp or a mouth organ from Johnny Fox.

Always the friendly ghosts of the past were here to meet you: Damn The Weather, Johnny Forty Coats, or poor Tom The Moon, ancient, ragged, wearing his indestructible grin. The kids dancing around him, screaming, while he mumbled some forgotten ballad.

"Oh, Tom! Tom! Show us the mooin."

* *hunger, famine.*

And when he took off his greasy cap to collect a few ha'pence, here was the moon, shining and hairless, and the squeals of the delighted urchins raining down around him like stardust from heaven.

If you were lucky you might come across a running gunfight with that famous gunslinger, Bang-Bang, who would take on half a hundred Indian kids, and Geronimo would bite the dust and die again in the sage bush of the Lousy Acre, Patrick's Park. And down the lost alleys of the Liberties and the lost years of your life, the acrid gunfire of the Coombe's only cowboy, the fastest draw west of O'Keefe's the knackers, would bring tears to your eyes.

In the Liberties of those days many of the men were returned soldiers who had survived the lunacy of Flanders but were a ha'penny short of a shillin'. One fine soldierly figure, for some unknown reason, used to go mad at the sight of Kevin Street police station. Something inside him would snap and he would step straight out into the traffic, ignoring the curses of dray and lorry drivers and, standing four-square on the cobbles, he would lob grenades, manufactured in his mind, straight into the station. The attack would be sustained until some guard came and led him away, and all was over until the next time.

On one unforgetable day Damn The Weather, Bang-Bang, and Shell-Shock Joe were all in the street together, the Weather Man damning a summer day with a lovely blue sky, while Shell-Shock, standing on some Vimy ridge of his mind, slowly and with dauntless courage attacked the police station. Down the road the Coombe's only cowboy had bailed up a dude gambler from Rathgar against the trees outside the public lavvo, and it was a case of "Claw sky, hombre", or be ventilated. The dealers, screeching laughing as a red-faced young copper just up from the country and not used to Liberties ways prevented Shell-Shock from earning another Victoria Cross, roared Bang-Bang on to shoot it out. The unfortunate gentleman from Rathgar who found himself in this menagerie, and who was transfixed to a tree, made a run for it as the cowboy threw lead. . . "BANG-BANG", as the whole street went mad and men, women and children went for their shootin' irons and dry-gulched each other in the dusty ravine at the bottom of New Street.

The Liberties, where beshawled women too broken for barrow work could be seen any day in the chapel, rosary beads in hand, praying to St Joseph or St Francis, or if things were desperate bad to the Blessed Virgin Mary herself, to intercede through her Son, for a little miracle that would put a bit of pig's cheek into their mouths; or made frantic by the want of another would boldly beseech the "makin's of a coddle. . . for the daughter, Sweet Mother o' Jesus, her fella is out o' a job, an' she has six childer. An' th'eldest is makin' her First Communion sooin". And throwing discretion to the winds they would promise to do a "special novena, Dear Mother o' Jesus, an' y'ill get her a new Communion frock, won't yeh?"

The crazy, heartwarming, drunken, poverty-stricken Liberties of my boyhood! The thieving, generous, brutal, kind, suffering Liberties of my youth. No wonder it was love-hate with me. No wonder I could never outlive it. So much viciousness, so much gentleness, so much Christianity that Jesus would have felt at home here. If fortitude and charity were the climate necessary for His love, surely then, on His second coming He would be born again in the Coombe: a Jesus with a Dublin accent!

The Crucible

I was twelve years old, the runt of all the gang; a terrible and paralizing inferiority complex was taking me over.

Just about everybody looked down on me, I was constantly reminded of my lack of inches, and it made life hard. And, God knows, life in the Liberties was hard enough without being small. The final indignity came when Kevin O'Toole, fifteen months younger than me, warned me for bumping into him.

"It was an accident," I sullenly told him.

"This won't be," he promised, bunching his fist under my nose.

I had had enough. If this big eejit got away with this, I might as well get lost. And walk in cowardice and fear thereafter!

"Right then," I said squaring up, and O'Toole, grinning, moved in. He, like my inferiority complex, was growing at a fearful rate and he was now ready to put his additional height, weight, and reach to the test. So was I!

I picked out a spot just under his left eye, ducked his guard, and let fly with a bony fist. He blinked and the smile went off his face. Before he could gather himself, I nailed him again on the same spot. Raging, he came at me like a bull. I let him charge past and when he turned gave him another ill dig under the eye. So far he had not even touched me. He backed away then, and I could nearly hear his lame brain telling him to take advantage of his height and reach, to box cool.

He moved forward deliberately, making little useless circles with the fist he was going to bury me with; I shot under the punch he telegraphed and struck again, viciously, on the bright red spot that had appeared on his cheekbone. He started to blubber then, and I could have walked away with honour. But the way of the Liberties was not the way of the Lord. Half the boys in the Square were egging him on. After all, if he could take me, they'd try too. I had other ideas.

This big, fat softie, the youngest of a family of about fifty girls, had looked for fight, and he was going to get it. Besides, if I gave him a real going over, the other ones who fancied their chances would back off.

"Come on, Son," I taunted. That was what his adoring family of sisters called him. He came again, turning his damaged side away, and I landed a beauty under the other eye. This was the Liberties: turn the other cheek and that's what you got. You got hit! And then I landed another heavy blow on the damaged side again. I had him! Now to teach the others what to expect.

At that moment the circle of boys exploded and Kevin's sister, a big sixteen-year-old shrew, fell on me like a rending fury. She grabbed me by the hair but I was too quick for her; I threw myself backwards onto the ground and kicked forward. She let me go quick enough then for I got her solid on the knee.

"Yeh dirty little maggot," she sobbed, "Teh kick a woman."

I rose, belted "Son" under the eye again, and swaggered off. But inside I was shaking. On the days that followed the O'Toole's doorway seemed always crammed with vengeful sisters waiting for me to pass. Things were bad. They would tear me apart when they got me. I took to going in and out via our back wall, on to the Back of the Pipes all the time now. Something had to give.

On the third day of my persecution I deliberately stood next to Son in line at school.

"Linda," he hissed, "'il flitther yeh. . . Gertie an' Nuala, an' Florrie 'ill bate yeh sick. . . an' me mother 'ill break yer face."

"We'll see whose face gets broken after school."

With that dire threat I left him. He tried to get away, but without a hope. It was a soft baby elephant run down by a jaguar. I was afraid to mark his face again, so I belted him twice in the stomach, and gave him the message while he bawled like a lost bullock.

"Every time one of your sisters hits me I'll hit you twice." Said with a set face and teeth showing.

Half an hour later I chanced across the Square. The Amazons were lined up in their doorway but, beyond glares of hatred, made no move to harm me. I had, Liberties style, solved my problem. Son would keep his place in future. His pals would keep theirs. Checkmate to his sisters. I had won a great victory. The crucible of the Liberties was hardening, tempering me.

But at the back of it all, the boy who loved to walk by clear water, and who told fairy tales, who could get lost in the beauty of a flower or a colleen's face. . . from somewhere that boy looked on and wept and was inconsolable. The iron rule of this place had been forced on me: "Never say your mother reared a gibber".

From now on I would live by it; and sore it cost me, from time to time, in the years to come.

The Granda's Secret Weapon

In his early seventies my Granda went into the export business and did well. All his life he had been a bird fancier, feathered ones only, and he was renowned throughout Ireland for the excellence of the canaries he bred. One whole wall of the top back room was covered with cages, each with three or four yellow birds, so that the place was always full of song. He had a fine voice himself and sometimes he would sing by the hour while he accompanied himself on the melodeon. That is how I remember him.

For years the Granda had had a secret weapon that had made him king of the canary breeders. Competition after competition fell before him, for there was no denying that his feathered challengers had a sheen of plumage and a gleaming elegance that was unmatched. He had discovered a food for birds that made them impossible to rival, a veritable caviare that they gorged themselves on if given the chance. Several weeks before competitions they were fed on this royal jelly of the bird world and, singing, downed all before them.

This carefully guarded secret was thistle seed! Every August the Granda collected it by the sack full when it was ripe. That was about three days before the thistle tops exploded and filled the air with flying paratroopers, a lethal seed that could, if it reached maturity unnoticed, give a farmer a lifetime of work. The Granda placed the thistle tops, whole, in the cages and left the birds to get on with the job. The room was always full of floating parasols and the Grannie, like Queen Victoria, was not amused. But, of course, the canaries took seniority over her.

It was one of my uncles who solved the problem of how to remove the seed from the thistle in quantity. The solution was simple and clever. The cog wheels and chain from a bicycle, plus one pedal, turned a timber wheel studded with rows of nails. When the contraption was operated these passed through similar rows of nails in the outer cover. The dry, ripe thistles, fed through an opening at the top, were torn to shreds, the seed tumbling out through a small hole in the bottom.

Selling this peerless product was no problem. His grandchildren, and they were legion, were bribed into frenzied activity in late July, and that first year he made over eighty quid, half a year's pay for a carpenter.

But directly across the road his enemy looked on with envy and hate. Old Scottie and the Granda detested each other, their feud rooted in some ancient quarrel, and all us kids had to swear on a prayer book never to reveal the secret of the machine. Scottie tried by every conceivable means to gain this information. All his moves and attempts came back to us! The house was vibrant with excitement, the Granda jubilant and triumphant as never before, his mortal enemy humbled. The whole thing took on the proportions of a Mafia confrontation. Let old Scottie struggle on his pension, the Granda gloated, he'd never break our oath of secrecy, never know the glory of a big cheque in the autumn. But he did!

Some louser who had access to both camps revealed all, and the next summer old Scottie had a similar machine ready to de-seed thistle tops.

"He'll never find the Scottish firm that purchased the seed," snarled the Granda, spitting bricks with temper. But he did.

Mind you, his firm never grew as big as ours, for he had not enough young grandsons, but he was the hated competitor, and if the Granda got wind of Scottie being seen in one of the places he regarded as his own then he assembled us in haste and we stripped it in an hour. The Granda would pick away, muttering inaudibly under his breath, and he was not saying the Lord's Prayer either. All old Scottie's movements were noted from the Granda's front room; he was tailed everywhere and in jig time we would strip another field – even with him in it! Scottie's fields, like stolen fruit, were sweeter to my vengeful grandfather and he would spend hours at home recapping events as another chapter was added to the saga. It was the same with Scottie, for he had his victories too, and the feud helped to keep these two old men vibrant with life.

And then, one autumn night, just after the big cheque had arrived, the Granny heard him sigh in his sleep and the next morning found he was dead. He was washed and shaved and made decent, while his pampered feathered friends in the next room hopped from perch to perch and sang delightfully in their rich, thistle-fed voices.

Presently old Scottie was seen to emerge from the tenement opposite, dressed in his Sunday best. We heard him slowly mounting the stairs, and then he was in the room, looking incredulously at the Granda's still face. Life would never be the same for Scottie again, and that day two Liberties export firms closed their doors forever. Scottie took off his bowler hat and, sighing, sat down heavily and faced the Granny. He ran a hand through his silver locks and a little sob escaped him.

"I'm sorry he's gone," he said slowly, "I really am."
It was the simplest and most heartfelt tribute I was ever to hear from an enemy to a fallen foe.

A Girl That Men Forget

In the mid-twenties the birds took over the dance scene: the red-red robin went bob-bob bobbin' along, blackbird said "bye bye", and the girls of Dublin took about two feet off their skirts and proved once-for-all that they did not go about on castors but had legs – large legs, dark legs, beef to the heel legs and, amongst the assortment on parade, many very beautiful legs. With the short skirts came short hair, the twenties "bob" with a fringe, and all over the world the long tresses of the fair sex fell softly to the floor. Things were never going to be the same again.

The avant-garde among women took to smoking at work, at home and in the theatre but for some obscure reason rarely in public; only the most abandoned among them ever did this, and they were universally regarded as "scarlet women".

"Brazen hussies," said my mother. "They'll be drinking and smoking, and wearing trousers next!" But even she did not think this last outrage would ever come to pass.

It was a time of sweeping change in attitudes, and during the summer of 1927 or '28 I became conscious of some small rebellion in my young old-fashioned mother. All the married women in the Square had had their hair bobbed and wore their skirts above the knee; their earlier outrage had given way to envy of the freedom enjoyed by younger women. The magazines of the day showed long-legged short-haired young women who had *it*. . . It being Hollywood parlance for feminine magnetism. My mother, sweating over a zinc bath and a washboard, began to complain about the weight of her lovely brown hair and grumble about the bun that chafed the back of her neck. She was a lone ranger now, the last of the Mohicans, the only woman around who could still sit on her long tresses, but she was conscious of the fact that she was made to bear this now intolerable weight, that she was not free like all her sisters.

My father made no bones about the fact that he was perfectly happy with her as she was. When the advantages of short hair were mentioned a dark glance or a frigid silence brought the subject to a sudden end. He took to singing an old-fashioned song which ended on a warning note: "When they say here comes the bride she will stand aside, just a girl that men forget". And he left no doubt that in his opinion it was short-skirted short-haired girls that men forgot. Quite often in passing he would swiftly kiss my mother, to show her she was the girl he would never forget, and she would blush like a schoolgirl and push him off with "Laddie, the children. . .", but her face would be radiant.

However, the storm gathered: my mother was under pressure, with all the forces of society against her, and one day, arriving home early from school, I walked into the horror of my mother's rebellion. She sat on a chair in the kitchen, behind her a woman who had been a hairdresser, and lying on the floor the shining coils that had been her crowning glory.

White-faced and trembling she afterwards drank a cup of tea with me. "Lar," she asked me, gulping, "What'll your father say? Do I look very bad?" Lying, I told her that she did not, but privately I thought that if my father's reaction was as bad as mine, then there would be hell to pay. I thought she looked incomplete, like a Manx cat!

I stuck around that afternoon as the clock moved relentlessly towards the time of his arrival home. We heard at last the sound of his bicycle being propped up in the hall, and then he was in the kitchen. For a second he stood in the door, disbelieving what he saw, then silently washed his hands and sat down at table. My mother placed his dinner before him with trembling hands, saying nothing, for there was nothing to be said. The revolution was a *fait accompli,* she had thrown in her lot with the rest of her sex and defied him. And, after all, if he had failed to hold the barricades against one wife, what hope had he now with the millions who were solidly behind her? This must have occurred to him as he ate his dinner in his quiet white silence. At length he rose and ascended the narrow stairs to the small front bedroom without a word. My mother was quietly weeping beside the fire, but it was only from the aftermath of the earthquake. The first great shock was gone, and anything else would only be minor ripples that she could easily handle.

The following morning I came down to the kitchen to find all as usual. Dad sat contentedly eating his breakfast; my mother was in the height of good humour and he kissed her fondly before he went off to work. The frantic mother of the previous evening was gone, and she gave me no explanation for any of it. I was sorely puzzled and spent hours that day wondering how such an earth-shattering event could be overlooked by my father, his iron command flouted.

I have, of course, long since figured out how my mother achieved the impossible, how women so often triumph, and how I lost so many similar battles myself afterwards. But that knowledge was still before me then, like the man with the wheelbarrow, and I went forth, like all the generations of boys before me, like a lamb to the slaughter.

Love, Joy And Peace

Long before the present bridge was built, before the canal that made it necessary was even conceived, there was another Dolphin's Barn Bridge, nearer to the Liberties. It was, and still is, at the junction of Cork Street and Dolphin's Barn, spanning a branch of the ancient Poddle which, long since piped, runs behind the houses of Emerald Square.

It was here as a boy that Johnny Forty Coats was pointed out to me, and apart from his colourful nickname there was little about him to interest a child. That he wore several overcoats was obvious, as was the can for boiling tea hung from a belt which held the first or the last of his overcoats together, and a sack holding all his wordly goods was slung over one shoulder. He must have been quite young when I first saw him, for his shaggy head of hair was as black as the old battered priest's trilby he wore and there was not a single trace of grey in the luxuriant beard. His real name was Watts and he was a quiet solitary figure who, as far as I was concerned, was not a patch on his brother Kit.

Kit Watts, younger than Forty Coats, was a wild figure with a shock of flaming red curls which must have been the envy of many a female. He strode through the streets in fine weather, stripped to the waist, sun-bronzed and virile looking, with an iron bar or a heavy ash pole over his shoulder, and the screams of the women shoppers when he erupted amongst them was a source of great joy to us kids. Fearsome as he looked he was quite harmless, though a ha'penny short of a shilling, and the local coppers regarded him with a tolerant eye and, I suspect, enjoyed the consternation of the women as much as we did. Kit lived on the Corporation dump that was slowly filling in the great hole left behind by the Dolphin's Barn brickworks, the yellow clay from which can still be seen in Dublin's Georgian houses and artisan dwellings. It was here that Kit Watts had built himself a hut from old corrugated iron and he lived, it seemed, quite happily with a few thousand rats. He died when quite young from rubbing red lead he found in the dump into a cut on his knee, and his picturesque form was sadly missed in the Barn.

Nevertheless it was his quiet brother who was destined to become famous all over Ireland, though had he gone we would never have missed him. But there were so many characters roaming the streets then that it was hard to travel any distance without encountering one of their number.

Damn The Weather was another colourful character who was quite capable, when among women shoppers, of creating even greater havoc than Kit Watts. He was a short, stocky figure, comfortably dressed, and wore a peaked cap. He would walk along quietly for any length of time and then, suddenly, as the mood hit him, his arms would be spread far apart and his hands would come together with a report like a rifle shot to the accompanying roar of "Damn the Weather". Women would scream and drop their shopping bags and there went the black and white pudding and perhaps a dozen eggs all over the path, while the Weather Man, placid again, toddled off, oblivious to the stream of maledictions that pursued him.

Even the shopkeepers then were characters, and our local grocer was known as "The Light Weight Champion of Dolphin's Barn". It was nearly worth losing an ounce or two to see him weigh a pound of bacon, the way the rashers barely brushed the white scales. "Like angel's wings," said the scathing Dublin women, "but they won't get him into heaven!" Nevertheless, inexplicably, the women continued to shop there, and he continued to rob them with his thistledown touch on the scales.

Money had its own peculiar "slanguage": a pound note was a "quid", half a quid was "ten bob", a half a crown became "half a dollar", a florin was "two bob", a "bob" equalled one shilling, a sixpenny piece was "a tanner", a "threepenny bit" was a "kid's eye", a penny was a "claud" or a "wing", and long before the Royal Air Force took on the Luftwaffe half Dublin got by on a wing and a prayer. Low in the scale a ha'penny was called a "make"; hence one unfortunate shopkeeper with bad eyesight was known as "Oul' Stare The Make" and indeed she had need to stare in order not to be bankrupted.

One of our number destined no doubt, as Dickens remarked, to die by suspension had discovered that Mercurial Ointment, rubbed well on a copper ha'penny could temporarily transform it into a gleaming imitation shilling, and naturally the lady with the poor sight came in for popular attention. It worked well for a while until she woke up and after that scrutinized every coin at close range, squinting hard, and forever became known as "Oul' Stare the Make".

There was a character, quite apart from all the others, who was known as "Love, Joy and Peace", and his message appeared all over Dublin. He was a small well-dressed figure who, armed only with some chalk, drew shamrocks on the pavements, each leaf holding its message for those who cared to look. "Love," said the left-hand leaf; "Joy," said the middle one; "Peace," said the last one. He had the face of an intellectual and the quiet assurance that comes from wealth and position. Nobody ever derided him, although all Dublin knew he was mad, but then the mob in Jerusalem two thousand years before had said Jesus was mad and his message was precisely the same as Dublin's pavement artist's. Certainly, in the gathering storm of the thirties his message never reached the hearts of Europe's leaders, with one exception, that gentle Englishman Neville Chamberlain, who was no match for the forces of evil he had to confront and, as

history records, was, like Jesus, crucified after his own fashion. Like the chalk shamrocks that appeared from the dirty pavements of the Liberties to the manicured sidewalks of Fitzwilliam Square, he was walked over, trodden down and obliterated in a couple of days, and forgotten by history.

The Fountain, James Street

In James Street long ago there was a picture house called the Fountain. It stood opposite an ornamental fountain, and there is this to be said about the picture house, that it was in no way ornamental. The seating was built to withstand hardship more than to provide comfort, benches of slatted timber eventually taking over from the much assaulted bucket-type seats, but this in no way prevented the place from making a healthy profit. The whole world it seemed had gone mad about the movies. It was my one aim in life to go to the Saturday afternoon matinee, and no errand was too much if it yielded the necessary pennies. But these were the poverty-stricken days of these islands: the prosperity of America's "Roaring Twenties" never came near and pennies were hard to come by.

The unemployed stood around on street corners penniless but somehow they managed to scrape the price of the cinema together, for in the warmth of the building they could forget for a little while the grim world around. Everybody sought refuge in the picture house. All the kids went to the Bowery, as it was nick-named, and the desolation of the empty streets of a Saturday afternoon was a thing to be dreaded. It was worse in summer, for one could not sit by the fire and pretend the matinee was not on, and the three hours when the gang would be missing stretched into infinity. The "followinupper" that had left the hero cliffhanging would have to be followed up at second hand, gloatingly retold by some kid who would assert, "Yeh missed it. . . It was the best ever."

How to avoid these traumatic occasions posed a problem, and the day I discovered that one could trade in a Baby Power or Jameson bottle for a ha'penny marked a milestone in my life. In those far-off days one could take a short cut from the Back of the Pipes to Rialto School by cutting through a huge market garden field and here I found prosperity, for it seemed that every drunkard in Ireland lurched along the same path, and most times there was a rich harvest to be gathered. With experience I cast my net further, figuring quite correctly that sometimes the bottles would be hurled away, and I found that an hour's hard work in the mud of the adjacent ditch yielded the price of the matinee.

But there was a snag. . . there always is. I was too shy to venture in to the pubs and trade. I had dozens of bottles hoarded and the doors of the Bowery were open to my touch if only I could get up the nerve to trade them in, but that I could not do. There was only one solution: to find a boy who had the nerve and split fifty-fifty. Regretfully I recruited Tommy Murphy who was not very keen on the idea, having rarely been to the movies, but after a couple of matinees he became a ferocious addict and towards the end of every week haunted me to make sure I came up with the bottles. For a while all went well. Tommy was a dull boy from a poor, dull family whose outlook was poverty-stricken, and who with no less money than their neighbours managed to be worse dressed and shod and fed than the rest. Tommy dragged his heels as he walked, hands in pockets, shoulders rounded in dejection, but Saturdays now saw the end of all that. We trotted happily together along the canal, headed for the screaming mob of kids and the Bowery, where some kind of order was maintained with the aid of a stick.

It took eight Baby Powers bottles to get us into the pictures and we were not coming up with enough of them; Edgar G. Robinson, George Raft, Pat O'Brien and the indestructable Cagney looked as if they would disappear from my life. I faced the prospect with despair, knowing that I need expect no sympathy from my mother, whose viewpoint was that "the pictures have the children of today ruined". In this she was backed by the priest and the Canon, who weekly slated the Hollywood imports. The pictures, it seemed, were a pernicious and diabolical influence on the young and we, the generation of the damned, were knee deep in mortal sins, too shop-soiled to care!

Came the Saturday when I had to confess to Tommy that I had only five bottles and that both of us could not go to the pics. To my surprise Tommy told me that we would go, that he had a few bottles stashed away himself, and took the five bottles and went off to trade them in. I watched him walk away quite cockily and suddenly it came to me how much he had changed. He did not drag his feet anymore, his shoulders no longer sagged and he exuded confidence. My dawning suspicion took root and that afternoon after a delightful picture about the St Valentine's Day Massacre I accused him gangster-style. "You double-crossed me," I told him, "You've been raidin' my concession."

And then before my very eyes the metamorphosis took place.

"Yeah," said Tommy showing his teeth in a hard Cagney grin, "Never give a sucker an even break. . . You'll have teh change, kid, if yeh want teh go places!"

"OK, wise guy," I said, narrowing my eyes to slits, Raft style, "You've just been included out of the act."

Thereafter, either as Raft or Cagney, I found the nerve to market my own bottles. Maybe the Canon and Mam were right, but not all the way. There was much good to be gained from Hollywood if you didn't go too far. That was my opinion and I stuck to it. I had to if I wanted to go places.

Dublin Turf-Cutters

In the summer that followed the bitter winter of 1947 Dubliners took to the mountains around them with something approaching the fervour of Moslems heading for Mecca. The mountains and their bogs offered the only solution to the threat of another arctic winter and around Sally Gap there was still plenty of bog to let. Accordingly, we took to the hills.

With my three brothers we took along an expert to instruct us in the ways of cutting and drying turf. As it transpired, he was from Dundalk and knew little more about the business than we did ourselves, but as long as he did not have a Dublin accent his advice found willing ears and he was granted the bogus status of a prophet. On that first misty morning he leapt out of the car, tore across the bog, ripped a small area clear of heather, and drove the sleán in. After going down about eighteen inches he laid the first lump of turf I had ever seen in its native state before our eyes, and pronounced it first rate.

"The best," he panted, like a prospector who has just struck it rich. "The very best."

Wild excitement all round, and we bent with a will to do the job of clearing off what your man called "th'ould scrawn". Nobody noticed that the mist had thickened, that it had turned piercingly cold and begun to rain. However, even as the gold-mad miner is forced to recognize the coming night, so we, too, eventually came to the conclusion that it was raining; indeed, that we were all soaked, and the sooner we left the bog to God and the mountains the better.

We repaired to the nearest hostelry at Brittas, where we decided that if we did not have a few hot "small ones" we would all be hospital cases. The man from Dundalk said we owed it to our young families not to get sick, and then got down to the serious business of making us bog experts. We had been blooded that morning; the stuff was there, it was dead simple to get it out. Indeed, by the time we were out of any danger of being hospitalized, the Louth man had explained all on the counter with a finger dipped in stout.

Outside, the rain came down like a waterfall on a sodden world, but inside all was hope and joy. The first cut with the sleán, it seemed, was known as a spit, and for my part I had gone down about ten "spits", had twenty tons of turf stored in the fuel shed and had sold two lorry loads for fifty quid each before I left the pub. All in all a very hopeful day. The only damper on the whole affair was the stout, which was a dismal affair indeed. Such was the demand for it in Britain that for the first time in living memory Guinness was in short supply and was being served in the pub before it was mature. The result was a black mixture, flat as a pancake and stale as a morning after the night before. However, in the interest of health we drank it anyway, and had the consolation of knowing that we would make no doctor rich.

The following weekend was a very different proposition. The sun shone down on the bog with never a tree for shade, all around us the toiling city greenhorns burned and blistered and stopped admiring the beauty of the mountains around midday. Quite a few of them were marked absent the following day and were never seen again. But it was no trouble to us brothers. We were all outdoors workers, used to all weathers, and we got the act together that day. Before it ended we had the pleasure of admiring the first rows of turf laid out to dry. Our hopes soared, even the flat pints on the way home did not depress us, though one customer acidly remarked that one could write a bad cheque with the stuff!

On Sunday we were all tired. The sun blazed down all day again, and around 7.45p.m. we wandered disconsolately off the bog, depressed by the knowledge that the pubs closed at eight. Even the long rows of turf stretched out did nothing to console us. My brothers slumped in the back of the car, tongues hanging out for a pint, too tired to notice that we were not headed homewards. I was driving and had had a happy thought. There was a little thatched pub I knew in a valley beside a favourite trout stream. It was barely possible. . . but it was worth a try.

In the dying sunlight the pub slept quietly at the bottom of a little valley, its thatch blazed golden, and a sheepdog dozed before the door. My heart sank a little even as I tried the latch, but the door swung open and I was quickly pulled inside. The place was packed! Every bog worker in Ireland had found it at the same time. The brothers were called in and soon we were gazing into the creamy heads of goodly stout – robust, mature stuff that was a fading memory in the city and only to be found in this Shangri-La of beer in the mountains. Blistered city hands picking up pints, capital-sized thirsts from the capital city demolished by these mug-punters of the bog.

An hour after closing time the publican raised a glowing face and addressed the man on the door.

"Lock that door," he roared happily above the din, "and let no customers out." A cheer followed, and then the crowd drank the little place out – wine, spirits, ale, the lot! By the time we finished the shelves were empty, the till full, and there were holes in all our pockets. Later our wives listened, but coldly, to our accounts of great quantities of turf drying out. Among us brothers the "bog talk" faded, the mining fever died.

As Dessy said to me in the Halfway House, "What the hell are we slaving away on the bog at weekends for, and no thanks for it?"

"Let them go cold next winter," I said morosely. "Don't know when they are well off."

My mother, however, took a different view when she got the four of us together.

"A right crowd of go-boys I've reared," she commented acidly. "Turf-cutters indeed. That'd be the dear winter's firing. Why don't you all club together and buy Donnelly's coal-yard? It'd be cheaper!"

"We were down three spits," Dessy told her.

"Indeed," said my mother. "Spitting in the sawdust is more in your line I think."

She squinted her eyes, gave us the hard smile she had for us when she loved us most, produced a bottle of whiskey and poured us four drinks.

"There now," she said comfortingly, "You all look more at home now!"

Keely For President

In the old days women were confined to the snug in every pub, a small partitioned-off area usually just behind the front window. It was a no man's land as dangerous as a mine-field, only ever entered by one man, the barman, who could be considered in the light of a medical orderly bringing first aid to the trenches.

That was long ago, when men gave up their seats on public transport to women and doffed their trilbies in respect, around about the time when the most brazen of the twenties flappers took to wearing men's trousers and called them "slacks". It was around this period that a character known as President Keely appeared on the streets of Dublin. He contested every election, and alongside the posters of Fianna Fail and Cumann na nGael came the information that Keely was running for president again.

These notices appeared all over the city, scrawled in chalk or painted, and when prominent politicians were to speak in public us kids made sure to be there for the bit of gas. President Keely, mounted on his orange box, would set up his own meeting in opposition to the politicians and would most times attract a larger audience. He had a positive genius for malapropisms and what are known in England as "Irish bulls". He had the colourful speech and accent of the native Dub and there was no avenue of fractured English that he had not explored and made his own.

He was quite mad, of course, but then derisive Dublin has always had a soft spot in its heart for such people and claimed that Keely was no worse than those who represented us in the Dail. The Civil War that had racked Ireland was only a few years behind and election meetings could be very violent affairs; Keely sometimes provided a welcome relief. He was a short, well-built man with a mane of snow-white hair that reached his shoulders, and he was endowed with the voice of a lion.

On the day I have in mind Keely in ten minutes flat removed half the crowd standing at the GPO listening to a national hero. He had set up on the corner of Abbey Street, only a few yards away, and was stating his programme for the improvement of the Irish Free State. One item, a matter of some urgency it seemed, was that once he was placed in charge of the nation's affairs the statue of Nelson on top of the Pillar would be made to face north instead of south. The reason given was that Nelson, that womanizer, had no right to be looking down on Daniel O'Connell, the hero of Catholic imagination. The laughing crowd roared its approval and applauded madly.

This was the Dublin that James Joyce knew so well, still squeezed in between the two canals, where most of the population lived in rooms instead of houses, a seething warren where poverty, by today's standards, was appalling. Thousands of children, summer and winter, roamed the streets and went to school barefooted, and

President Keely's next proposal, for the provision of boots for footless children, was greeted with uproarious approval. Every minute the crowd increased as the national hero's audience melted away, drawn by the laughter; by now the hero was nearly talking to himself.

When the President spotted some boys clinging to lampposts laughing at him he opened up again. The youth of today, he roared, had no respect for their elders, but he'd fix that by opening a few more reformatories. It was not the mothers and fathers he blamed so much as the parents!

The crowd went wild and cheered madly. Encouraged by this Keely went on to say that if them boys were in Russia they'd be "thrun" in the Liffey.

"Law and order has broken down," he claimed, "An' yeh won't believe this, but when I came out of the pub last night, there was me bike. . . gone!"

Across the street the Grand Central Cinema was showing *Hells Angels,* starring Jean Harlow, the first of the platinum blondes, and Dublin just then was full of peroxide imitations. Apparently, Keely did not approve of this and, glaring at the picture house, he announced that he was sick of "palatic" blondes. As regards the women who were wearing men's trousers, they should go to the chapel, see the priest, and ask him to "concentrate" them.

At this point the Gardai moved quietly in to break up the meeting, as Abbey Street was completely blocked, the crowd spilling half way across O'Connell Street. The President, on his orange box, spotted them first and shouted that "a crowd o' polis men" were about to interfere with the right of a citizen to speak in his own city.

"I'm a Dublin man," he roared passionately, "Born an' bred in this town, an' if God spares me I'll be buried in Glasnevin."

Dubliners who remember President Keely must be thin on the ground now, and those who do are getting on a bit. His reign was short, spanning only a few years, but it was sweet. He disappeared off the scene quite quickly and I never found out what became of him.

Unless he changed his name he never made it to Leinster House, I'm nearly sure of that, but in the times that were in it he would certainly not have been out of place. Indeed, he would pass for normal today, of that much I am very sure. Keely for President? Why not!

"Ruggy Up"

Although there was much Christian charity abroad in the Liberties of fifty years ago it could also be a place of violence. People who lived in the frightful conditions of the tenements, many families sharing the one toilet and water tap, often rubbed each other up the wrong way, and feuds developed. Saturday night often saw one of these feuds reach its peak, and the bottled-up frustration would be settled in the street between two determined men, who were usually far from sober. It was a bare knuckle affair, there were no intervals between rounds, the contenders just getting stuck into each other until honour was satisfied. A bare knuckle fight is no joke, though usually little serious damage was done. The whole affair had a well-established routine. When the row erupted in the pub the whole crowd spilled out onto the road. There was little traffic. A couple of burly buckoes with swinging leather belts established a circle, look-outs were posted for coppers, and the fight began.

It was then the familiar cry would fly from Patrick's Street to Dolphin's Barn in a matter of seconds.

"Ruggy up," went the cry, "Ruggy up!"

The first boy who saw the crowd forming would shout the news and run towards it. The next boy within ear-shot was duty bound to shout before heading for the scrap, for "Ruggy up" meant just that: a fight.

The bush telegraph of the African jungle, although aided by witch doctors, black magic and drums, was snail-like compared with the Liberties equivalent. Boy after boy would shout the glad tidings and take off. Very occasionally some eejit, bored by an unnaturally quiet Saturday night, would start a false alarm, but the first boy to hear the shout would always be able to identify the culprit and, as the kids converged on the pub, milling around from all over, and it became obvious that the call was bogus, the hunt for the culprit would start. Boys who had raced half a mile in record time and then faced the desolation of a peaceful street were not easily placated. The bored one had shouted that there was a fight, and a fight there would be. Even if he escaped justice that night he would be summarily dealt with the following day, and that lad would remain unpopular for a very long time. He had only to open his mouth afterwards, on any topic, and someone would close it for him. He would become a pariah, a maverick outside the herd who belonged nowhere. He had desecrated the sacred code and Judas Iscariot, by comparison, was an honourable man. He would never do it twice.

There was one pub in particular that stood head and shoulders above all the others for the quality of its brawls. It was at the meeting of four streets, a crossroad not far from the public lavvo in New Street. The coppers from Kevin Street never got near any of its fights; the look-outs could see too far in every direction. And here on Saturday nights men settled their differences squarely, in public. There was never any dirt and there were no bovver boots in those days. Karate chops and kicks were unheard of; to be caught in possession of a brass knuckleduster could get you killed, and these men, if it ever occurred to them, thought of knives as something belonging to Latin America or southern Europe.

The fights were strictly Marquess of Queensberry

Rules: no punching below the belt, a fair fight fought to a finish. The next morning the opponents of the night before, sporting black eyes, would often be seen drinking and laughing together about the fool a man could make of himself in drink, and how a few "small ones" could drive him half mad. Of course, as everybody knows, the Marquess of Queensberry was completely mad, and without half the cause of the residents of slumdom. These men who fought on Saturday nights lived in conditions calculated to drive a saint mad, a life deprived of all privacy and human dignity. It is as well to remember that harsh reality when listening to someone wax nostalgic about the Liberties in the "good old days".

Recently I went again to the cross where the fights used to be. The pub had long since gone, along with most of the people. All the tenements, thank God, had been demolished. But a lovely new row of tastefully designed houses had sprung up in their place, homes for a new generation of Liberty Belles, and the old bells of St Pat's sounded as lovely as ever. The once swarming pavements were, by comparison with the past, deserted, but in my mind's eye I could see again a horde of ragged boys running from all quarters to the rallying cry of "Ruggy up". The red-jerseyed bowsies who fought fairly here seemed, in retrospect, manly, even gentlemanly compared with the pavement "mugging" thugs of today, for in those days beating up old folk was something that happened on Mars.

Poverty, they say, breeds crime. I have not seen a ragged backside or a boy in bare feet for years, but when they were a dime a dozen one could walk from the north side to the country on the perimeter of the south side without fear. For all its poverty, dear old dirty Dublin, my home town, was in many ways a lovely place in which to live.

3
TIMES PAST

The Passing Of The Clydesdale

In the social hierarchy of the Liberties the publicans were at the top. Next to them shopkeepers jostled for position, and third were the tradesmen, bakers, carpenters, bricklayers and others. Lowest of all were the labourers, with one exception: the labourers who worked in Guinness's. They were in a class all their own, never knew broken employment, and worked with the conscious air of belonging to the world's largest brewery. They were privileged above all others, Guinness's being light years ahead of the usual employer of those times.

Workers' children had a Guinness Clinic where sickly kids received toffee-like extract of malt, lovely stuff! They had free dental care, and if a child was hospitalized they convalesced in a private Guinness Nursing Home. Nobody could live in the Dublin of long ago without being conscious of the presence of the monolithic brewery, for chugging up and down the Liffey, all day, came the fleet of shallow barges that ferried the barrels of stout downstream to Dublin Port. They were colourful chunky little craft that threw up clouds of smoke and made a great fuss about their job. They had a high funnel that was on a hinge, and it had to be lowered going under the bridges of the Liffey.

Guinness's horse-drawn drays, pulled by huge Clydesdales, rumbled over the cobbles of the city delivering the national beverage. At the Spring Show Guinness put on a magnificent display: four of their biggest horses, brasses and harness shining, oak barrels gleaming on an immaculate dray, plodded their stately way around the arena on blackened hooves. The drivers, all big men, sat on a single seat high above, wearing bowler hats fitted with chin straps against the breeze, and moleskin jackets. Florid of face, proud of their gleaming horses, they advertised the fact that Guinness Stout was food for man or beast. Rumour said that the men and horses drank a bucket of stout a day – each.

The bargees and the horsey men were the elite of the labouring classes but they were, alas, even then under threat from the growing force of the new fleet of motor lorries. On a summer's day on top of Dolphin's Barn Bridge I watched a Clydesdale come to grief. The tar-covered roads of those days had an unseemly habit of melting in hot sunshine. As the horse lumbered over the bridge, bracing his back legs against a heavy load bound for the pub just below, the enormous hooves started to slide forward in the melting tar, and in seconds the Clydesdale was sitting on his rear, firmly embedded in the road.

A derisive crowd of kids soon gathered to see a Guinness's horse sitting up like a dog, the red-faced and embarrassed driver the recipient of quips that could only be thought up by a Liberties crowd. It was more than an hour before a squad of men arrived from the brewery on the back of an empty dray. The barrels were swiftly transferred and then the whole gang went to work to extricate the unfortunate Clydesdale. They unyoked him and by main force got the animal back on his feet. The horse left the bridge with a horrible squelch and left a hole in the road that was now glued to his rear. The crestfallen driver led him away.

It had all been great "gas", one of the memorable incidents of my boyhood, and I followed the driver and horse, for they were going my way. Rather than run the gauntlet of the Barn and Cork Street, the driver went home down the Back of the Pipes, a right of way leading all the way to the brewery, and I sauntered behind, watching lumps of Dolphin's Barn Bridge dropping off the horse, in fits laughing but careful to keep my distance from the infuriated driver. That is the last memory I retain of the great Guinness Clydesdales. Very soon they were gone, disappeared into the realms of folklore.

Later, one of the mechanical monsters that had wiped them out came to grief on a similar hot day in the same place. Applying the brakes on top of the bridge, a bus skidded at speed in the melting tar and went straight into the pub at the bottom of the slope. By some miracle nobody was killed, or even injured, but only the back of the bus was visible, the rest being embedded in the bar. The publican nearly had a stroke, though rumour had it that the driver climbed coolly down from his seat and, sighing philosophically, said, "Ah, well, I suppose seein' as where I am I might as well have a pint".

Stranded Sailors

For a couple of centuries the Grand Canal, on Dublin's south side, contained the city in a tight liquid band. Up to the thirties the capital had never dared to cross Dolphin's Barn Bridge. Once over that it was all fields, and through them flowed the clear watery highway.

The man who had first dreamed up a canal had thought of it in terms of cheap transport, of a horse being able to pull by boat much more than by wheel on land. He did not think of it, I feel sure, in terms of being a source of endless delight to fishermen and young boys, but so it turned out. It was to the Herbiton Bridge, then in deep countryside, that we swarmed out of the Liberties to learn to swim.

Our hated enemies from Cork Street scored heavily here, arriving with blown-up pigs' bladders from Donnelly's bacon factory which they used as water wings.

They learned to be unafraid quicker than we did, but there was no help for it. They were many, we were few, though for reasons of recreation the undeclared truce at the Herbo was never broken. The canal was the only thing cheerfully shared, but we were never stupid enough to go to Cork Street for swimming aids.

Even then the decline of the canals had already started. The barges had put up a spirited resistance to the railways by becoming motorized, but they could not resist the road-eating lorry and they soon started to die out. World War II came just in time to save them for a time. Diesel oil, chronically scarce, went further on water than on land, and the canals came back with a bang which was really only a dying kick, for seven years later it was all over.

On Mount Street Bridge one day I watched a barge coming through the lock. "Ay, skipper," roared an idler, as if an ocean-going liner was passing below, "What's yer cargo?"

The skipper, a red-eyed man who looked as if he had been dragged off a binge by the imperative of sailing, glared back. "A load o' whores," he ground out. "Come an' see if yer oul' wan is among them."

The idler informed him that the oul' wan was dead and he didn't like whores, "But bring us back a parrot from Culchie Land, Captain, will yeh?"

The incensed skipper roared that if he was ashore he'd give him parrot, feathers an' all. This last remark was liberally laced with what our American cousins call cuss words and was delivered in a Dublin accent even better than your man's on the bridge. It was a striking example of the true Dubliner's talent for invective, words even being hyphenated to make room for others. His grasp of profanity was awe-inspiring, almost an art form, and nothing like it will ever be heard outside Ireland's capital. London costermongers are boring by comparison, with their constant repetition and lack of imagination. And the skipper was nothing unusual, just an ordinary

Dublin gurrier at home with his Muse! Lady street traders were his natural sisters, and some of them could blister the paint on a door at fifty yards with their tongues on a cold day. Few of them, however, could better the skipper.

The canals reached their late zenith in 1945, and the stretch that used to branch off at the first lock and finish at James's Gate was never busier. From the builder's yard where I worked the barges passed all day, low in the water coming, empty and high above it going back. For it was mostly a one-way traffic. The neutral capital, its great port idle, had little to send. The country, as always, had plenty to give, and Guinness had never needed more grain, or the greedy city more turf.

On a furious March day the wind shrieked as we doggedly worked at the benches. Cigarettes were scarce, money even scarcer, but between three of us we raked up enough for a few fags. The apprentice was told to chance the pub on the corner. It was beside the harbour, sheltered by the monolithic buildings of the brewery, a place of echoing footsteps and still water. Shoals of striped perch passed under the tiny metal bridge in water as clear as gin. And this in the heart of Dublin!

The apprentice came back grinning, told us the pub was full of stranded sailors, and that the publican didn't serve kids. So when the foreman turned his back I slipped out. The harbour was crowded with empty boats and all along the canal, known as "The Gut", the barges were securely tied up. The pub, as the kid had said, was crowded with stranded sailors, and as the publican grudgingly sold me six cigarettes I asked with a straight face what was wrong.

I was told by a contemptuous sailor: "Yeh couldn't hould an empty barge on course in a high gale." Any eejit, he implied, would have known that – except, of course, a Dublin one. He was waiting for this jackeen to grin and make a smart crack. I did neither, the ferocity of drunken sailors in port being well known to me from my reading.

That stretch of canal is only a memory now. Grass grows where the barges rocked that windy day, and storm bound-old salts who had faced into many a southwester on the wind-scalded plains of Kildare sombrely sipped their pints and sampled the quiet flesh-pots of James's Gate. Young trees send down roots where my striped perch swam. After the canal was allowed to silt up they filled it in and called it progress. But some idiosyncracy, some quirk of nature in me, refuses to agree. Nothing that takes so much labour to create and is so beautiful should ever be allowed to disappear.

A Close Shave

In the days when the cut-throat razor ruled supreme going to the barber's to be shaved was an everyday affair to many of the Liberties residents: comfortable men, traders, shopkeepers, business men. Chins well lathered, they casually discussed football or horses or the latest from the Dublin music-hall scene, snippets about Jimmy O'Dea at the Olympia or Aleck Friar at the Queen's, perhaps a bit of scandal about the chorus girls, relayed by a man whose sister's daughter knew the wardrobe mistress's nephew's son. . . stuff straight from the horse's mouth!

There were usually two or three barbers working close together in these small shops. Many of them were bird-fanciers, and captive canaries sang to a captive audience from cages hung on the wall. The shops were impregnable fortresses of male supremacy. Women were barely suffered to enter with their sons for first haircuts, and then only in slack times.

As always, like everything else, it took me a long time to aspire to a manly growth. Everything about me seemed reluctant to enter the world of men. I was only four feet ten until I was over sixteen and then, in a frenzied paroxysm, I shot up to my full height of five feet four – in my shoes, that is. I was destined to be a small man, but at least I made it. However, it seemed as though I would never grow a beard. Fellows who had been three or four classes behind me at school were sporting blue-black chins and five o'clock shadows and here I was, well into my twenties, with not much more hair than a gooseberry, scraping my face daily with one of the new-fangled safety razors, more in anger than in hope, to encourage face-fungus fertility. I longed to take my place among the men in the barbers. They had nothing but contempt for safety razors and said women used them to shave their legs.

"They'd be linin' up in the barbers if they could," said one, "Brazen hussies who are startin' teh wear men's throusers in public. I'd like teh see my dhaughter thry it!"

It seemed ages, but eventually the day dawned when I deemed my beard fit for public execution. At last I would savour the luxury so obviously enjoyed by my compatriots, the whole manly ritual from the first lathering with the soft-hair brush to the voluptuous delights of the hot and steaming and ice-cold towels, alternately laid on; I would emerge into the street with a shining, tingling, rejuvenated face! It was all before me.

The barber I got was new to the shop but not to me. The last time we had met was at school where I had done him a mischief; I'd given him a black eye for calling me a runt! He greeted me civilly enough.

"Howayeh, Johnny," I grunted, manly Dublin style.

"Yew won't take long," he said maliciously, lathering me.

So, I thought, as he turned to greet the next customer, the dig in the eye still rankled. Then he was back, gleaming blade in hand, leaning over me, breathing heavily, intent. At the first touch of the razor's edge I stiffened and held my breath, but had to release it before I suffocated in a mighty gasp. He jumped back and for the benefit of the shop said resentfully,

"Don't jerk like dat! Be another t'ing if I cut yeh!"

His face had an angry flush, and over the white sheet that was tucked under my chin I could see one baleful eye – the one I had closed – fixed intently on my exposed throat as he deftly pushed my head back and started to scrape away. And I had a sudden dreadful vision of him going beserk, of the bottled-up hatred of me taking over, and him doing a "Sweeney Todd" on me. The old-fashioned melodrama I had sniggered at on stage suddenly came alive with a vengeance and once again I heard the demon barber's ferocious chuckle, and the whining "Can I do you now, sir?" as he murdered his client; the chair tipped backwards, the trap-door in the floor opened and the body hurtled through, later to be served up next door in meat pies. . . and sweating through every pore it was all I could do to keep sitting. It was only the fact that the shop was crowded that stopped me from running.

At length I emerged into the street, shaved, hot and cold towelled, face dusted with powder, but in no way rejuvenated. Shakily I headed for the nearest boozer and a stiff drink. After two double whiskeys over the pint chaser I could see, quite clearly, that I was. . . well. . . not wholly wrong. . . but I could be a little in error in my earlier cogitations about females and shaving. I mean, there was nothing wrong with the safety razor, even if women did shave their legs with it. I supposed that they had been pulling the wool over men's eyes for centuries, for before the razor blade hadn't they used pumice stone for the same purpose? And anyway, there were enough men knocking the fair sex without me adding my fourpence worth.

And then, to be honest about it (and there's a lot of honesty in two balls o' malt and a pint) I came from a long line of cowards, civilians to a man for centuries, careful people with not one ending up in a Sweeney Todd meat pie. Too cagey, like me! But there is this to be said of cowardice, and of me personally: my breed live long, hang on to their front teeth to the envy of the others, and die in bed.

Sheffield Steel and Tortoiseshell Combs

I have always had a soft spot in my heart for the old-fashioned "short back and sides" barbers, and the one I presently attend is among the last of the Mohicans. He is a valid throwback to the old days when barbers' shops were full of song, for the walls of their tonsorial emporia were always festooned with bird cages in which much-pampered canaries sang all day. They bred their own birds and entered all the competitions, and the barber who won the much coveted "Best of Show" award stood high among his contemporaries. The whole tribe of tonsorial artists seemed knee-deep in feathers, and one only had to praise their birds' quality of song or plumage to make a friend for life.

Barbers were a friendly, talkative race, and their ability to keep their victim in the chair in conversation was regarded as part of their trade. Alas, those days are long gone, and their simple shops have been replaced by glittering unisex salons where Mister Teasie-Weasies shampoo, blow dry and permantly wave long-haired lovers from Liverpool. "God be with the days," I say regretfully, and wouldn't be got dead crossing the threshold of one of them. Indeed, I might prove a grave embarrassment if I did, for time has long since blow-dried most of my hair away.

The only time I entered one of them was with a young

nephew, and the experience soured me for life. Suave, ultra-efficient young hair stylists attended their clients, male and female, whose needs seemed to be the same, God bless the mark! I staggered out of that establishment and to regain my mental equalibrium headed for my old-fashioned barber where I could listen to the crack and didn't have to have a hair cut if I didn't want to. And my thoughts went back to all the barbers I had known and their simple song-filled shops, and I hoped they were all in heaven, where feathers are all in the fashion.

I had rejected up-market establishments in my youth, with their odour of expensive aftershave lotion and cigars, and had gone across the Liffey to where the king of all Dublin barbers daily held court. His was a most extraordinary place, much favoured by down-to-earth men, reporters, professional golfers, trout fishermen, and the average Dub who likes the colourful life. Hubert was a small man in a small shop that had a pot-bellied stove surrounded by a wire guard in the middle of the floor. The guard was needed, for in winter the stove glowed red and the canaries never knew a cold day. Hubert left the doors of the cages open and the birds flew about at will in their tropical paradise. Hubert had been involved in "the Troubles" and as a consequence had many pictures of that period hanging on the walls between the cages, and the birds built nests of human hair behind them. To assist them in their task Hubert had come up with the idea of cutting up bits of string and dropping them amongst the hair on the floor. The birds soon copped on and used the string to reinforce their nests behind the pictures. Whether they ever hatched out their eggs in them or not I never discovered, but nest in them they did.

As I sat in the barber's chair before the gleaming mirror I experienced a very real sensation of looking in on two other people. Hubert stood poised behind me, scissors held aloft, comb in hand, saying in his soft, unctuous voice, "Well, sir; now, sir: I think we have come to know each other. Not too much on or not too much off, and a touch of the Robert Taylor about the side locks, I believe."

"Yes, Hubert," I'd say happily, for to be addressed as "sir" at nineteen is a heady experience, especially when it comes from a man old enough to be your father. Sometimes for devilment I bull-baited him with pretended ignorance about the true facts of the Troubles and Hubert would throw up his hands in horror at the ignorance of the young "scut" in the chair.

"Good heavens, no, sir," he'd exclaim, "What schoolmaster taught you your history?"

The day I told him Arthur Griffiths had been stabbed to death in Harcourt Street he nearly had a stroke. I insisted I was right, though I knew full well that the late great man had died in bed. I had often seen fellows being barred from pubs but I had never heard of one being barred from a barber's; I came near it that day.

Hubert had little time for the young generation of barbers who were following in his honorable footsteps. "No manner about them, sir," he'd tell me, "No conversation, no style. . . nothing! Now, in my day you did your seven years on the floor, went to Tech, and if you passed your final test you got your white coat, your Sheffield scissors and your tortoiseshell comb, and Bob's your uncle, you took your place among the men. Mind you," he would add, "I don't know what the combs were made of, but that's what they were called. . . tortoiseshell!"

Sheffield steel and tortoiseshell combs have long since ceased to dominate the market but, like Hubert himself, they remain in the mind as marks of excellence.

Matt's Mine

In these times of government schemes to encourage our youth to launch their own businesses I cannot help reflecting on the entrepreneurial skills it took even to survive in what was the Irish Free State. My friend Matt Thomson was a born survivor. He was brought up in a hard school, learned early that the world did not owe him a living, and if he has not yet become a millionaire he has never yet had to hit the trail for foreign parts either. In Matt's household pocket money was unknown and he, being addicted to Western movies, had to find it somehow. To get fourpence for the Saturday matinee he dug gardens, mowed lawns and clipped hedges out Ballsbridge way. At twelve years of age he was already a seasoned campaigner, and when war broke out Matt came into his own.

Early in the conflict it was decided to turn Dublin's Ringsend Park over to growing vegetables, each family to receive one-eighth of an acre, to alleviate the shortage. It was here Matt once again took up the spade. Part of his willingness to turn farmer was his concealed intent to sell off some of the crop in order to go to the Ritz picture house, known to all as "the shack". A "shackless" Saturday afternoon was hell on earth to Matt.

Ringsend Park was on land reclaimed from the sea and, like all tip-heads, was composed of the city's rubbish. Almost anything one could think of was there, quietly rotting away beneath the earth covering, and almost at once the allotment made all Matt's dreams come true. His spade uncovered a vast amount of coke cinders, dumped there by the local bakeries – Kennedy's,

Boland's, Johnson, Mooney and O'Brien's – who used up to eight tons of coke per day. The cinder wastage was enormous, and Matt stood on top of incalculable wealth for Dublin was desperate for fuel of any kind and coke cinders mixed with turf made a good fire. All that was required was to mine it, and without any government aid at all the Matt Thomson project was born.

At sixpence a sack he found a ready market and his Saturdays at the shack were assured, not to mention such luxuries as illicit Woodbines, chocolate and ice-cream. Suddenly he was the richest kid around. No more mowing lawns for peanuts: the big time beckoned! All Matt's spare time after school was now divided between mining and deliveries, which he did in a home-made box-cart. He was in business, sentiment played no part, and even his granny had to pay the going rate.

And it was the same resentful granny who encompassed his downfall. The hardest part of the enterprise was sorting through the cinders for foreign bodies such as small stones and slate, but with the lush lifestyle Matt now enjoyed the sorting became careless; avarice had crept into the act, and complaints of exploding pebbles and flying cinders became frequent. Like many a world heavyweight champion who had slogged his way to the top, affluence was proving too much for Matt and he was growing soft.

Things suddenly came to a head on his next visit to the granny.

"You'll bring no more clinkers here," she screeched, "Yer last lot blew th'altar lamp teh bits, an' the cat got hit an' hasn't been seen since. Wait 'till I see yer father!"

She did not have to see his father. Her complaints were heard far and wide, and the next day the intrepid miner was hauled to the surface by a horrified park attendant; the mine, now nine feet deep, closed forever.

"Stupid little gurrier," said the attendant. "He could o' been killed if the bank collapsed. All the same," he added, "Yeh have teh admire the go in him. We could do wit' a few more like that around here."

Dirty C On St Patrick's Day

It was St Patrick's Day in 1940 and "Dirty C Company" of the 7th Dublin Infantry swung proudly over Portobello Bridge. In one of the army's toughest battalions, C Company had earned an unenviable reputation. They couldn't even play soccer decently, hard chaws who'd sooner kick the man than the ball! Dirty C: mutinous mid-city products to a man, today we glittered as we marched with tens of thousands of our comrades in a show of strength. We were putting on record, for the world to see, our determination to defend our neutrality. If any of the major powers *had* attacked we would have been quickly wiped out. We were armed with rifles that were older than ourselves, wildly inaccurate, with pitted barrels, and nearly as dangerous to us who fired them as they would ever have been in the field. Perhaps more so, for they kicked like a mule and, incorrectly held, could break your jaw. But they looked well, and we with them.

My beloved cousin Freddy, at five feet seven, was three inches taller than me, but it was recognized that we marched together, and after the sergeant had gone through the complicated drill that placed the tallest at the head and rear, the shortest being in the centre where I always found myself, Freddy loused up all the sergeant's good work by slipping back to me, our pals doing a swift double shuffle with expertise.

Right now, Freddy was four ranks in front, next to my late enemy, Gallagher. Gallagher was a brilliant boxer whom I had often admired in the ring. He was a regular soldier, too, a bully who always picked on the least able in the latest batch and gave him the mother and father of a hiding. I was the softest-looking touch in our lot and, wearing the distinctive uniform of a volunteer, constituted a double affront. My accursed long eyelashes had betrayed me again. Usually the trouble they caused was nice trouble, feminine trouble, but this "get" was out for blood – mine! I was scared stiff! I avoided violence and only fought when cornered, like a rat. But a rat is a dangerous little beast and I was no exception. Behind the saintly face and the long eyelashes was a Liberties product; I had almost completed seven years of carpentry and was as tough as whipcord, even though I looked a pushover. Gallagher took to calling me "girlie" and jostling me; I stuck it for days, then bluntly told him to "lay off".

"OK, kid," he said, "You're for it!"

For a week I avoided him, suffering cold meals. This man could take me apart and I knew it. My only hope, I figured, was psychological warfare, and my moment of truth came soon when the whole Company was confined to barracks because of dirty bed-boards. I was so frightened I kept out of the washhouse, hiding behind it, trying to wash the boards in a basin of water. I was too scared to face Gallagher, but I was going to do it nonetheless. *Never say your mother reared a gibber:* the iron law of the Liberties!

One pace over the washhouse door, and Gallagher tapped me on the shoulder. I stood there in slacks and singlet looking as cool as a cucumber, but inside I was shaking. I was also as white as a sheet, an ominous sign if only he had known. He danced around, limbering up, and warned me to get my hands out of my pockets.

"What?" I said contemptuously. "For a slum bird like you?"

And that was it, the psychological bit. His face flamed, the dancing stopped, and he telegraphed a haymaker. I ducked under it and hit him with all the suppressed fury of a week's humiliation. I hurled him back, realized I could hit him again, and did! The washhouse was about fifty feet long and I punched him from one end to the other. I gave him no chance to recover. I opened up all his boxing scars and he ended up pouring blood over a sink.

His regular army pals came then and put him aboard a stretcher, with him promising terrible revenge when he was patched up; I knew he could do that, too, for I had only caught him off balance. As they carried him past he jumped up and struck me. His pals saved him from retribution that time, but I sneaked over to the doorway and belted him full in the face as he went by. More psychological warfare, and I made my mark that day and was accepted at last, long eyelashes and all. A man who would hit another on a stretcher was worth watching, and my tactic worked for he never came at me again, and the rest walked around me.

But right now we were soldiers together, row long forgotten, marching to the skirl of the pipes through our very own city. I was only twenty and what the hell did I care for anything except the little mots who would be watching out for me! Let the war clouds gather, let them all come – the Germans, the English, the Aussies and Canucks. Me and Dirty C and my gleaming old rifle that could kill if you got close enough: we'd take care of them all. And with our ancient Lewis guns that suffered from more stoppages than CIE we'd mow them down!

England, Home And Beauty

Coming in out of the freezing north of England blackout I stood there blinking, taking stock of my new lodgings. A poor, untidy home, but the blazing coal fire made it lovely. Over the mantelpiece hung a cheap, tasteless print and beneath it on a chair a kitten was contentedly washing its paw, like a little hand with a furry glove on it. Above all it was warm, and the ugly old man rising to meet me, with his watery eyes, big red sponge nose, his clown's smile and his whole good nature displayed by his ill-fitting dentures, was the warmest thing of all. James Barnes, of 22 Uniform Terrace, Warrington, Lancashire. Night watchman! Dogberry! The nickname was irresistible.

"Good evening," I said shyly.

"Eh, lad, I'm right glad to meet thee." We shook hands. "Meet missus," he said with pride.

The tall old lady tidying the table smiled. "Married a young 'un, I did," she said, "'e's only sixty-eight, an' I'm seventy-one."

"I can hardly believe it," I said and, really, he looked far older than his wife.

"'E's me third," she said.

"I were married afore, too," said Dogberry defensively.

"Only once." She pointed a finger. "'Im an' Ted Earls were after me for years. Said as I'd marry first one back from war. 'E were back first."

While she was making tea I studied Mrs Barnes. Tall, stooped, withered, with apple cheeks and a pair of enormous, luminous, hazel eyes that would coax the birds out of the bushes; it was easy to imagine the devastation she had caused when younger. This was the widow, then, who had sent two men into the hell of Flanders to win her favour, and Dogberry, by my reckoning, must have been over forty then. And I could see by the manner of his introduction that poor old Dogberry was still mad about her.

"You're Irish," she said flatly.

"Dublin," I said defensively.

"Dublin, Belfast, or Cork," she answered, "I wouldn't know t'difference. You're all t'same." I felt ashamed for, sitting there in my six-guinea Burton's best and my suede shoes, I thought it was obvious I was a Dublin City man, and she had just said we were all the same.

"You're very small for an Irishman," she said, hitting me on a sore spot.

"I am, Ma'am," I said swiftly, "But there's smaller than me where I come from. Everybody over here thinks an Irishman is seven feet tall, with a long upper lip and a shillelagh under his arm, an' the little divils dancin' in his laughing Irish eyes."

"My, my!" Mrs Barnes interrupted. "You're Irish right enough. Smart an' fiery. You'll do. I like a young fella to 'ave a bit of go in 'im. 'Ad a proper meal today, lad?"

"No, Ma'am."

"Mrs Barnes 'll do," she said tartly, "I'm not t' queen."

"Eh, lass," said Dogberry fondly, "Thou art t' queen of this 'ouse."

She shrugged his hand from her shoulder impatiently and Dogberry, like a faithful old watch-dog who had been kicked, subsided in confusion; his light went out, the smile was gone, and all that was left was an old man who had been too often rejected.

"Got food ration books, Paddy?" she asked.

"I have, Mrs Barnes."

"Good. Three's better nor two. I'll go down t' food office in t' mornin' an' fix up."

"An'," said Dogberry, suddenly glowering, "Thee'll not be wearin' thy good 'at! An' thee'll not be talkin' to Ted Earls! I 'eard all about thee last Sat'day mornin', talkin' an' makin' up t' 'im. Whole street were skrikin'!"

And there and then she did the little jig I was to see so often afterwards.

"Me," she said derisively, "Makin' up to 'im? I could 'ave 'im any day I lift me little finger."

"But 'ee'll not 'ave thee," Dogberry shouted ferociously.

"Ah," she said jigging her way to the pantry, "Shut up."

We had tripe and onions for supper, and we talked a lot before I went to bed and Dogberry to work.

It snowed all that night and, through the bleached hell of a freezing building job, I worked the following day, thinking of the new digs and Dogberry and the poverty of their slapped-up council house, and the unfaltering courage of the old man.

"Eh, lad," he had said, "Old 'itler is playin' merry 'ell wi' us now, but we'll get 'im! We'll get this lot, too."

We had grown quiet then, listening to the drone of the German bombers flying over to knock some more "merry 'ell" out of Liverpool. The guns opened up, uselessly, into the thick cloud from the gasworks close by and the jerry-built house jigged, almost as much as Mrs Barnes had done. From the heaped-up fire a small avalanche of red-hot coals spewed over Dogberry's slippers, and with a roar like a lion he stumbled up.

"Bastards," he shouted at the ceiling. "We'll get thee."

And then the fit of coughing took him; his raised fist was clenched white with the silent paroxysm, his red face purpled as he fought for breath. Old Mrs Barnes, apparently delighted with this diversion, jigged up and down while I hastily shovelled up the smoking coals. Gassed in the last war, old Dogberry.

"Got whiff from Kaiser Bill," he told me, after order had been restored and we waited for the bombers to fly back. They came faster then, one more load of death lighter, the laboured hammering gone from their engines and the guns doggedly opened fire again. While the racket was on I studied the trembling print over the fire-place.

A tall, horse-faced aristocrat in a captain's uniform strode towards a mansion. On the steps a wasp-waisted beauty with a long skirt and a plastic face awaited him; beside her, two little Harry Whartons with shining eyes watched their Pater, with his arm in a sling, fearlessly crossing the Axminster lawn. Underneath were the words: FOR ENGLAND, HOME AND BEAUTY!

Ireland, I thought fervently, you're not the only one who is rearing them yet.

Dogberry looked at me with affection as the guns grew silent. "Eh lad," he said warmly, "I saw thee lookin' at picture. That's a grand picture, lad, a right good 'un. Thee'll not 'ave seen the like in Air." (He meant Eire.)

"No," I said civilly, "I have not."

"A grand lad, 'e was!"

"Who?" I asked in surprise. "Him?"

"No, no. But 'e were like 'im. . . were captain. Our captain! Got 'is lot in t' Battle of Somme. Shot through lungs."

He took out an old Bruno tin, opened it, took out some papers and started to roll a smoke. The little kitten, who had been hiding in terror, crept back and started cleaning its other glove.

Dogberry laughed wheezily. "Eh, lad," he chuckled, "We 'ad some times, we did. . . me an' t' captain. . . an' t' lads."

He lit his fag, drew on it, and started to choke and turn purple again. Across the fire his wife jigged in time to his coughing.

"You should stop smoking," I said kindly when the convulsion was over.

"Aye, lad, suppose ah should. Were only comfort we 'ad in trenches, though. Captain smoked Turkish, 'e did. Aye. Me an' t' captain 'ad rum. Bought it hisself, ower his own pocket, for t' lads. 'E were like that. We were all suppin' up, while barrage were on, an' when guns stopped captain took last swig from bottle. 'Quietly, now, lads,' he whispered, 'Follow me.' An' ower top he went, wi' us after 'im. . . eeee," he said, his voice tailing off as he gazed down the trenches of the years.

And I had a sudden, dreadful vision of Dogberry, past his best, swallowing rum among the shivering young boys, peering into the dark and the muck and the sheer bloody lunacy that was Flanders. For England. . . Home. . . and Beauty!

"Took three trenches that night, we did, wi' 'and-grenades an' cold steel. Old Jerry don't like cold steel," said Dogberry. "But 'e were too foxy for us that night. 'Ad company lined up be'ind. . . an' that were t' end of us."

"How many of you got back?"

"Me. . . an' t' captain."

"Thought the captain was shot?"

"So 'e were, lad. But not bad. It were the cold that killed 'im." He looked at his swollen feet, relaxed now out of the crippling boots, and sighed.

"Me an' t' captain got out. Lay in shell 'ole all night, an' t' next mornin' 'e were dead, an' these" – he raised a foot – "were frost-bit. Been playin' up ever since."

I had gone to bed then, and Dogberry to work.

Now, chilled to the bone, the day was over, and the whistle blew. Overhead the sullen clouds, loaded with snow, were bringing an early night. . . a good night, I hoped, with no Jerry upstairs and twelve hours' respite from the cold. The light was off as I let myself into Number 22, and Mrs Barnes was sitting in front of a roasting fire. The place was clean and shining, and a starched cloth covered the table.

"Took us by surprise, you did, yesterday," she said.

I smiled. Around her shoulders was a beautiful old lace shawl, and her silver hair was lovely in the firelight.

"Where's Dog. . . Mr Barnes?" I asked.

"Won two quid on 'orses," she replied. "Said as we'd sup ale tonight. 'E's taken a fancy to thee, lad."

"You're looking very glamorous tonight, Mrs Barnes," I said, slipping her the old Blarney. "And I'll go halves with the ale."

"No. Thee'll not go 'alves: 'is treat; 'e wouldn't like that." She smiled, delighted. "'E wouldn't like that last remark, either: 'im catch me in t' dark wi' 'andsome young fella like you. Switch on light, lad."

I did so. "Why," I said jokingly, "is he a terror?"

"'E is, lad. . . though never wi' me. Best 'usband in t' world. But you don't know 'im. 'E never finished story of 'im an' t' captain last night. 'E won Victoria Cross."

"Who? The captain?"

"No. Jim!"

"The Victoria Cross!"

"Aye. Jim carried captain ower no man's land and hid in shell 'ole. Covered captain all night wi' 'is own greatcoat, 'e did. Snipers 'ad them pinned down. Then when captain died 'e come out of shell 'ole screamin' an' charged Jerries on his own. Killed sixteen single-'anded. Our lads 'eard 'im screamin' an' came ower t' 'elp. Jim were cut to bits, an' gassed a bit, an' 'is feet were frost-bit. . . an' that were t'end of war for 'im. 'E never told me anythin'. It were Ted Earls told me, after."

"And that was when you married him?"

"Aye. . . in t' 'ospital. 'E were home first, an' I'd made promise."

I caught the glimpse of tears in her eyes, and looked away.

"Only man I ever loved," she said softly to herself, "were Ted Earls."

Dogberry came in then with a glow on, the pockets of his overcoat bulging with bottles of insipid mild beer, a bag under his arm with more in that and the sweet smell of Jamaican rum on his breath.

"Eh," he grinned, "I'm right glad to see thee, lad," and shook hands again.

Mrs Barnes nodded significantly. "Rum again," she said. "Dinner's nearly ready."

While she was looking after the meal Dogberry produced the evening paper and rustled it importantly, put on a pair of wire-rimmed spectacles with one glass cracked, and sat down. Over his shoulder I could see that things were going badly for the British. Singapore had fallen and some young reporter with stars in his eyes had written a mighty banner headline:

JAPANESE OCTOPUS SPREADS TENTACLES
OVER FAR EAST

Mrs Barnes sat down, and I could see that this was part of a well-established ritual.

"Read news before dinner, lad," she said. She smiled. "Jim's a scholar, 'e can read."

"Ah can that," said Dogberry proudly.

"'Ow's war?"

"Bad, lass, right bad. Lost Singapore we 'ave, an' Japs is spreadin' their testacles. . . ower Far East! Our generals, lass," he said seriously, "are makin' balls of war, but don't worry: in t'end we'll get 'em."

He put the paper firmly from him, locking the black news out of his mind. Mrs Barnes stood up to serve dinner and slipped off the lace shawl.

"That's Limerick lace," I ventured.

"Aye," she said. "It were my grandmother's. Got it from mother, she ran from famine in Ireland. . . she were always right poorly. Died when I were only five."

"Then you're Irish?"

Dogberry chuckled. "Aye, lad," he said proudly, "This family is 'alf Irish. Married a colleen, I did."

After dinner we sat around the fire and supped ale, and I whipped around to the pub when I was out the back and bought a half bottle of black market rum to liven things up. I sang "Danny Boy" and then Mrs Barnes sang "She Walked Through the Fair", and sang it perfectly. Dogberry, transported with delight, decided to give us his comic number. On the second time around I knew the chorus, and he and I bawled it out together.

We packed up, an' away we went
It's cheaper to move than pay the rent,
All we left for landlord was 'alf a pound of starch,
An' Saturday morning, without warning,
We were on the march. . .
Were on the march, were on the march,
Were on the. . .

The guns opened up again and we were abruptly silenced. Overhead the German bombers flew a familiar course, engines labouring for Liverpool. Dogberry heard it first, the misfired conk-conk-conk of a plane in trouble, and flung himself on the floor.

"Down!" he roared. "'E's in trouble; 'e'll drop bloody lot!"

And then it came, the blood-freezing sound of bombs

whistling through the night; the explosions close at hand, the front door blowing in, the lights going out and, in the tingling aftermath, the desolate sound of falling glass and the wailing of children.

"Are thee all right, Jim?" came Mrs Barnes's voice from the dark.

"Aye, lass. . . are thee?"

"Yes. . . Is Pad all right?"

"OK. . . OK," I said from under the table.

Dogberry struck a match. "We'll 'ave lights on again in no time," he said confidently. "Take more than old Jerry to put out lights in Warrington."

Three minutes later the lights were back. Swearing softly, Dogberry scrutinized the picture over the mantelpiece and picked a piece of glass from the plastic beauty's bodice. He sighed his relief. There was no more damage. He found a hammer and some tacks in the kitchen press and grinned.

"Good job I sole me own boots," he said.

All the bombs had landed in a waste lot about four hundred yards from Uniform Terrace and only superficial damage had been done. Together we jammed the front door back into position, and I started to tack newspaper over the holes in the window; Mrs Barnes swept up and Dogberry piled coal on the fire until it started to grow warm, and then it was time for him to go to work. With the bombs had come the snow, great heavy feathers already covering the scars in the waste lot.

He sat down, grunting, eased off his slippers and painfully forced his feet into the boots with the knife slashes. Mrs Barnes was strangely quiet as she handed him his sandwiches and torch. Dogberry kissed her, and this time she did not shrug him off.

"See thee in t' mornin' lass," he said fondly. "Goodnight, lad; look after missus for me," and he left by the back door.

As I tacked up the last of the paper I watched the old man come out from the side of the house, braving into the bitterness of a Lancashire winter in the big boots with the slits for his ruined feet; his wheezy goodbye from his busted old World War I chest. And then I had another look at the gallant hero over the fire with his gallant wound and, Lord Jesus, I swore to myself: England, Home and Beauty!

I watched him wave from the gate, shoulders already white, and march off into the night with hope in his heart and a great confidence in England. And I envied him, for I was lost. I envied his courage and the courage of his fallen friend in Flanders; I envied his tawdry ikon over the warm fire; I envied the gallant hero and his plastic beauty. I envied the two little Harry Whartons, probably up there right now chasing the bombers back over the channel. I envied everything and everybody, for they had come to terms with life, as it was, and little neutral me. . . I had not!

4
DIFFERENT WAYS

Herring Gulls

As a mid-city child I often stared up at the soaring seagulls and envied their ability to look down on the tall Georgian houses that I subconsciously hated. I did not like the gulls so much when they screamed raucously from the rooftops, heralding bad weather, but in Stephen's Green feeding the ducks my dislike of them took firm hold. They came out of the sky, dive bombing the ducks and, scattering them in panic, greedily took over. I noted their cruel hooked beaks and glittering yellow eyes, and felt afraid.

Dublin was a small city then and mostly the herring gulls sought their food in Dublin Bay, but even then a few had discovered the growing city dumps, where they fought ferociously for scraps. Now it is estimated that on Lambay Island alone there are forty thousand gulls which pose a major hazard to planes flying into Dublin Airport. Inevitably there will be a disaster if their numbers are not controlled, but more of that later.

They have already been responsible for one major catastrophe in my life, and Dublin trout anglers, in particular the ones who are growing long in the tooth, will know instantly what I mean. As a young man I had often fished the King's River before the dam was built at Poulaphuca creating the huge reservoir that swallowed a whole mountain valley, and the sorrow I felt that my favourite river had gone was very real. As the valley slowly filled up I often looked at the growing lake and wondered how the small brown trout were faring in their new home. It was three years before the ESB permitted anyone to fish it, but when a few like myself tried it the results were spectacular. Unable to keep our secret, the news got around and uproar followed. The little trout of the King's River roaming freely over their new pastures had prospered and grown fat. Here, on Dublin's doorstep, was the greatest trout fishing lake in Ireland. Three pounders were common, seven pounders not unusual; nothing like it had ever been recorded before. The gold rush started but like the Klondike it was only the fit who could hope to reach this fishy Eldorado.

All this happened during World War II and there was only one way to get to the lake. That was by bicycle. Petrol was strictly rationed, the buses few, and the long seventeen mile ride from Dublin was by way of the rising embankment outside Tallaght, a kind of Celtic Chilicoot Pass that was sometimes littered with spent Dubliners, either resting or mending burst bicycle tubes. However, for those hardy spirits who made it the rewards were rich. In one night's fishing I caught six trout weighing nineteen pounds. It was only at night that one could fish without being spotted by the wily trout, and a large fly resembling a White Meadow Moth was deadly. A catch like this was par for the course, but it was too good to last.

The engineers who had been so successful in bringing water and electricity to Dublin had made one fatal mistake as far as fishing went. They had overlooked a small pond, high on the valley's side that teemed with undersized perch. These had also found their way into the lake, where they provided a good meal for hungry trout but somehow managed to survive, however precariously.

The seagulls, meanwhile, had over the years been penetrating further and further inland and, all too soon, night anglers began to be alarmed by loud splashing around their feet, and the dawn would reveal a monstrous trout lying dead beside the shore. Experts were called in and all fishing was suspended while they tried to unravel the mystery of the reservoir's dying population. Eventually they discovered it was the gulls that had spelt death to Ireland's greatest lake. Flying over the water they sometimes defecated, and it was in this exercise that the fatal explanation lay. Their excreta contained a parasitic organism that found its way into the trouts' food chain and, attacking the liver, brought about the death of their hosts.

When the lake was re-opened things had changed. The spiny-backed perch had multiplied by tens of thousands, and now the few trout left were no longer the hunters but the hunted. One evening I caught a three pound perch which held six fingerling trout. There was only one thing to be done now, and that was to introduce pike, who would thrive on the perch and perhaps give the trout a better chance, and somebody did this. But the great days were gone forever.

As regards the airport's problems with gulls, their numbers could easily be controlled by culling their eggs in the nesting season. These eggs are already available in the city – blackmarket, of course – and fetch a high price among gourmets and the hotels who cater for them. The eggs are larger than a big duck egg, with mottled green and white shells. I was given a present of half a dozen of them a couple of years back and ate them with a vengeful angler's delight. They are delicious, with a rare delicate flavour, but that is the only thing delicate about the screeching, quarrelsome herring gull. If you can't beat them, eat them.

The Ferret Lowry

A long time ago, before Dublin became the "inner city", when there was no "outer" city, our family moved into the green fields of Crumlin, where we immediately started to destroy our new environment. We could not help that, for we lived by building houses. Most of our employees were from the Liberties, but now I became aware that we had a small percentage of an entirely new breed: the County Dublin man. We had a couple from Ballymount Lane, one from Crumlin Village, and two more from the slopes around Old Bawn, wild mountainy men from barely charted territory.

They were all very much of a kind, lightly built men who seemed to be made of sinew and whipcord. From the very first I tried to curry favour with them. At lunch hour they spoke casually of things that left me breathless, of badgers and foxes and rabbits. They spoke of their ferrets as a southern plantation owner might speak of his slaves, without love but as if they were just short of being human. Some needed to be starved before they would work, others needed to be fed before the hunt or they would kill quickly and sleep in. Still others would only work in tandem and refused to hunt alone.

There seemed to be no end to the quirks and whims of these pink-eyed prima donnas of the underground mutton world. Although at first sight I hated them I now began to see if I could learn a little of the lore possessed by these men so that I could go hunting too, but how to get them to accept me? I was the boss's son and therefore suspect; I stood on the other side of the barricade.

It was my heart's desire to go hunting with Jack Lowry from Crumlin Village, known as the Ferret Lowry because of a certain sharp-nosed resemblance to the creatures who aided and abetted him and his undisputed superiority among men who hunted. Unfortunately, he was a communist which in his simple terms meant that he refused to enter the tiny village chapel – a little gem and the smallest in Ireland – and he detested men like my father who made money out of the sweat of workers. The problem of how to get around him seemed insoluble until I found out he was "fond of a drop".

Many a morning after my father got the job started he would leave me to check any materials that arrived, but my main function was to dock the time of the late arrivals. The Ferret was always among them. After all, a man who has hunted hard all day Sunday and flogged a dozen rabbits for drink on Sunday night can hardly be expected to show willing on Monday morning, and so it came to pass that the moment my father left the job the Ferret started to work – at least, according to the time book he did. We came to understand each other in a hurry, and my Sundays with him became days of wonder in the worked-out sandpits around the far-off wilds of Walkinstown.

The Ferret handled the creatures he was called after with the casual dexterity of a baker handling dough; his hand just went into the sack and out came a squinty-eyed killer blinking in the sun. If it balked about entering a burrow it was rammed in and another one after it. His own kind never turned on him! He was a king among men and I walked proudly in the shadow of greatness, hero-worshipping him as only a lad can. I imitated him, of course, and on his request to "Give us a ferret" I boldly thrust my hand for the first time into the sack, where one of the murderous little brutes immediately met his teeth in my little finger and had to be belted off.

My hero regarded me with something bordering on contempt. "Yeh could o' killed the animal," he told me scornfully, "Y'ill never make a poocher if yer afraid o' ferrets." I could have told him after that that it was a moot point who was most afraid of the ferrets, the rabbits or me, but I kept quiet and took to wearing heavy leather gloves. But I lost face with the man I admired so much, the one who taught me more real lore of the ditches and fields than any other.

I never did get used to the bloody business of "poochin" rabbits, and now I know it was a youthful love of the hunt, the freedom of green fields, the delight of escaping from the seething city that I was celebrating. I had no love of the kill but the Ferret Lowry took the whole cruel business in his stride. Why would he not? This was the way of things in the village. His father and his father before him, and others before that again had lived this way, and sometimes depended on the ditches to provide the day's dinner. For centuries their tiny village had provided servants for the Lords of the Pale, and in earlier times a man like the Ferret might have been hanged or shot or deported for doing what he now did so freely; poaching rabbits.

That is all a long time ago now, but in my mind's eye I like to see the Ferret Lowry again, on a Sunday night in the Shaw Arms in Crumlin Village, as it used to be. He, flushed with success and a "drop o' the crathur", reliving another day's hunt and flogging a rabbit for one and sixpence. I do not like to think what I and my breed did to him and his village. War and famine and pestilence had not succeeded over the centuries in killing his kind or his place, but we builders finished the pair of them off. We buried him and his fields and his sandpits under a tide of houses, not a slow creeping in of the sea like at Merrion, but a sudden furious tidal wave that engulfed the village and all the wild roses that bloomed in the fields of Crumlin. County Dublin men who hunt with ferrets must be thin on the ground these days, as Dublin city eats its own county. Around Crumlin, of course, they have been extinct since the Ferret Lowry died, and that's a few years ago now.

A Pocket Full Of Kisses

Old Christy Quinn sighed, squinted through bare branches at the wintry sky and put the letter from Australia back in his pocket. So, his daughter's marriage, never happy, was finally finished, all washed up, and now he had two little grandchildren who had no father. Always a no hoper he had finally "snatched his rent, humped his Bluey and shot through", which, translated, meant that he had drawn his pay, packed his case and deserted his wife and kids.

It was lonely for her now and she was wishful to come home. It would be lonelier than ever for himself this year, coming up to Christmas, and he was getting on; not old, not by any means, but "kicking on a bit", he admitted. In this day of Our Lord, three score years and ten was not worth talking about! Why, he had read of a valley in Russia where everyone who was anyone was over a hundred years. At seventy-one he was only an apprentice.

"But if that is so," said his mind, "why have all your old friends gone? Have they all taken up residence in Russia?" He smiled and patted the cat. "Fluke," he told the purring little animal, "the truth is that I am getting old and I won't admit it."

There, the truth was out, but with it came no peace for it presented another problem. Was he making up his mind to pay his daughter's fare home because he loved her, or because he was afraid of the coming darkness? Was he giving all he had because the shadows grew daily longer?

"Fluke," he said to the cat, who was luxuriating on a Palm Beach mat before the hot Florida fire, "I'd hate to think that!" The spotless tabby yawned, sat up and started to wash its face. It was infinitely graceful, he thought, but then most young things were. "I wonder what the other two daughters are like, Fluke?" he said aloud. For answer the cat rolled over on the mat, belly up. "So that's your answer, is it?" said Christy. "Like yourself; young!"

Talking to himself again, he thought; the sure sign of loneliness. One he knew, from a photograph, was a piquant-faced charmer aged five; the other, the baby one, was a blur. Like most men all babies looked the same to him, except black ones or Oriental ones of course. If he decided, this day, to bring his family home, he had a lot to learn in a hurry. Did the airline charge for babies? How much: half fare or full fare?

"Sweet mother of God," he said to himself with rising panic. This air fare, together with the extra room he would have to put on his cottage, would just about clean him out in the bank.

Against the soaring background of the Sugar Loaf mountain, starkly outlined against a leaden winter sky, the cottage opposite looked warm and lived in. A young woman was putting the final touches to a Christmas tree and now the fairy lights flashed on to the delighted screams of her two children. Santa Clause was coming, a bit on the early side Christy thought, with Christmas Day still three weeks away. "But, still, kids. . ." he mused. He'd have the same problem himself in the years to come. Jem Mac opposite had his daughter and two grandchildren living with him, another broken marriage, with old Jem the winner. Jem's cottage looked kind of different from his. He groped around in his mind and then came the word he was seeking: cosy. Warm, lived in.

The front door opened now and a little girl, snugly dressed in a red coat with a matching tam-o'-shanter and scarf, ran out carrying a saucer full of breadcrumbs. She was going to feed the birds again, and his eyes lit up as a cheeky robin without fear lit on her arm and started to peck from the saucer. From the open door came the sound of a recording, lovely and clear on the cold air. "Silent night, holy night," and the reedy voice of the little girl feeding the birds came with it.

He shivered. It suddenly seemed a little chilly in the warm room. In Jem Mac's opposite there was warmth and light and love, and here in his lonely home the only thing that glowed was the fire. In three weeks to the day it would be the twenty-fifth, Christmas Day, and he would have a sore head. Every Christmas Eve he went out to the local pub; he went out early and returned late.

Normally he scarcely drank at all, it was just that Christmas Day got under his skin. He convinced himself, and anyone that would listen, that Christmas Day was just another day to him, but that was not true. Year after year it was an intrusion in his life, reminding him that time was passing and that life was passing him by.

He picked up an old pair of field glasses for the window ledge, focusing them on the child, and grinned, suddenly enchanted. He could see every tiny grimace of the earnest face as she struggled to reach the top note, mouth open, showing two gaps where her real teeth were coming through, her eyes screwed up, reedy voice off key, and suddenly, as the child's mother came through the door with her fingers in her ears, laughing, he found he was crying. He put down the field glasses and sat on the sofa, silver head bowed as, for the first time in thirty years, a storm of grief swept over him, bringing the tears. He had not cried like this since his wife had died, long ago, on the birth of his only daughter. He had never re-married; he was that kind of man.

Presently he raised his head and gave the cat a watery smile. "Getting old, Fluke," he said. "Tears and Christmas. I'm over the hill." Maybe he was, but wasn't there supposed to be a new and different view over every hill; even this, the last one? Well, what was the view?

"It's what you make it," said a small voice inside him.

He looked across the road again and saw Jem Mac, well muffled up in his wheelchair, take his accustomed place inside the glass porch. His grandchildren clustered briefly around him, then started the serious business of the day – games on the lawn. Old Christy picked up the field glasses again and focused them on the face of his lifelong neighbour. He was very old and tired-looking today; he hadn't worn as well as the Quinns, Christy thought. Whatever his future in this life, he had more of it before him than Jem. Maybe God had been a bit hard on him in the early years, taking the missus, but in the heel of the hunt He had atoned a bit by sending him a winter of perfect health; he was slowing down a little, that was all.

The garden, with its well-tended lawn and beds of wallflowers ready for spring, did not reflect the passage of time. His vegetable plot at the back with its crop of winter cabbage for sale did not show tired work. He was, he reflected, a comfortable man. How comfortable would he be after he had built the extra room and paid the air fares? He felt the rising panic again and fought against it. He would be flat broke, his mind told him, with nothing left but his old age pension.

"Sweet Mother of Jesus," he prayed, "Guide me. Tell me what to do."

"You know very well what to do," came the calm answer. "You don't need me to tell you. And as regards having nothing you are already a rich man. You could be richer if you were not afraid, rich in love and the happiness that comes with giving."

"It's just that, like Samson, I'll have lost my hair, my little bit of security that I've saved hard for. . ."

"And has my Son ever seen you in need? Perhaps He has not given you all you wanted, but you have always had what you needed. Is that not so?"

Of course it was.

"Well, then, why not go forward unafraid?" asked the quiet voice.

Across the road the little girl with the missing teeth had fallen into a rose bush and scratched her hand. She was weeping now and old Jem had his arms around her, comforting her – as he would soon be able to comfort his own grandchildren if he made a decision, and he need never weep alone again. To hell with the money, for that is where all money belongs anyway, he thought. He would wire off the fare that day. His daughter would get it and his telegram tomorrow and be here for Christmas. He could have a daughter and two lovely girls to love, and no more Christmas Eves with drink the only escape. All this wealth he could buy for a few lousy quid.

Now there were Christmas decorations to be bought and put up, streamers with flashing tinsel and a small pine-tree to be carried home and festooned with presents. So much to do, all of a sudden; what an adventure it would be to have children under his roof!

Six months ago he had placed a piece of silver in the hand of Jem's daughter's latest and had gazed in wonder at the perfection of fingernails, translucent as tiny pink seashells. To see the world anew through the innocent eyes of a child, to be part of its formation; to tell it fairy tales and watch eyes grow round in wonder at a lemonade stream with chocolate banks! To watch the grimace of distaste as Mickey Snider the horrible spider and his terrible companion Sneakin' Thomas the dirty white rat planned a banquet – of fly stew and mouse steaks, no less! To hear their laughter as this nasty duo got their comeuppance, as they always did. What times he would have! He had better start practising stories on the cat before they arrived; he must have grown a little rusty at the fairy tales over the years.

"Fluke," he told his pet, "You are about to be introduced to fairy land."

He patted the purring animal and reached up and took his cap off the hook; he pocketed the bag of sweets he always kept in the house and went outside.

A few flakes of snow were falling softly and the children, wildly excited, were noisier than usual. Twice he called them but no one heard him. He stood then in the middle of the cul-de-sac, took off his cap and flung it with a roar of mock rage on the ground.

"Does anybody want any sweets or not?" he demanded fiercely. "One sweet for two kisses." The children came running then.

"You've put up the price," said Mary of the missing front teeth. She had quite recovered from the rose bush. "That's not fair," she objected.

Old Christy gave her a crafty grin. "It is fair," he said snappily. "The price of sweets has gone up too an' I've me a profit to make the same as the next!"

"Oh, well then," she conceded. He knelt down to receive the moist kisses on his weathered cheek, handing out the various assorted sweet bribes for sweeter kisses.

"I suppose y'ill get on the gargle Christmas Eve," Jem called across to him.

Old Christy drew a line across the top of his bottom set of teeth with his forefinger and grinned. "Only up to there, Jem, that's all," he called back.

But that would not be true, not this year, for there would be no pain to kill. He stood up suddenly, scattering the children who fled in mock panic, roaring about his stolen sweets, tearing the paper bag into bits and scattering the paper confetti over the delighted kids. Four miles away the Sugar Loaf mountain was etched blackly against a sky that promised snow and far down the road the Wexford bus drew near, headed for Bray. There was a bank there and a travel agent, and he had business with them, urgent business. The bus drew to a halt and the doors opened.

"Comin' near the festive season, Johnny," said Christy to the young conductor who only yesterday, it seemed, had been in the line for sweets.

"It is, Mr Quinn," said the conductor. "An' in case I don't see you before then: a happy Christmas to you."

"An' the same to you, Johnny, an' many of them."

Yes, he could feel it in his bones. This was going to be the most wonderful Christmas of all.

A Room With A View

It must be lonely at times to be wealthy, to be made to endure the isolation that money can buy, especially when one is ill, for despite a national health service it is in the field of medicine that the greatest discrimination is to be found between the very wealthy, the voluntary health contributors, and the ones who have to rely on what is generally known as the white medical card. This is no fault of doctors, surgeons or nurses, who give the same care and expertise to all. It is something a capitalist society has forced upon hospital boards. They need money, and lots of it, to run hospitals; the wealthy have it but demand the exclusive privileges which only money can buy. It is a sad thought that a poet, with a golden heritage to bequeath the nation, may die without the trappings of honour, while a shady character with an eye for a flaw in a deed or a loophole in the law can command a private room. Money talks, and never louder than now.

All the old Dublin hospitals have had new luxury wings built and have seen their gardens disappear under avalanches of bricks as the city's population has exploded. Sadly, most of the hospitals are due to be relocated well outside the central city area, and with their departure will go the last of the thirty-patient wards, where the beds are docked side by side like small boats after a storm, the washed-up flotsam of the city's tide. This is where you will find the white medical card holders, in the main cheerful and all the better for the comings and goings of doctors, nurses and the cross-section of humanity that surrounds them.

In such a ward I watched a world-famous writer pass quietly across the Jordan, a man who had written one unforgettable novel which afterwards made millions as a movie. Inflation had probably caught up with him in his old age, or perhaps he had not studied the fine print in his contracts closely enough; whatever the reason, he was not wealthy, but anyway he would probably have opted to die among the working-class folk he loved so well. He did not die alone in that exclusive crucifixion for which the rich pay so much.

In such a ward I found, in the bed next to me, an old

music hall artist who had spent a lifetime on stage and, improvident as becomes his breed, had gone through a large fortune on slow horses, fast women, cards and drink; now he played his last card, the white medical one, and, entertaining to the end, regaled me with tales (when he was well enough) for many a pleasant hour. Together we walked down the ghostly corridors of dead theatres that came alive again with his voice. He had played the same bill as George Elliott "the Chocolate-Coloured Coon"; he had once seen Marie Lloyd; he had known a galaxy of English stars who had been greatly loved here. "If they could make it in Dublin," he told me, "they knew they were made!" He gave me, too, a glimpse of a capital city ruled from abroad, where Irishness was frowned upon, and he spoke of Sackville Street, where no decent woman would walk on the GPO side – the soldiers' side! He gave me a quick personal look at the world of my father which even Joyce could not have bettered.

On another bed lay an old lamplighter who had worked for half a century putting sparkling sequins in Dublin's midnight black hair, who had come from the dim gaslit days of his youth into the glare of the late twentieth century. Starting with a bike, a ladder and gas mantles for replacements, progressing as electricity took over to carrying light bulbs; switching on power manually and winding time clocks, until the photocell activated by fading light took over and his day was done. He was perceptive to a degree and told me something I will never forget: that the "Mary Magdalenes" of Dublin looked "more at home" under gaslight! He enthralled me, and there were many others who did the same. There is a lot to be said for the old, allegedly unhygienic wards.

How much of one's recovery may be due to the proximity of such company has never been weighed in the balance against the loneliness of a private room. Perhaps one day soon they will invent a computer that can do just that, and its findings may well bring the multi-bed ward back in a hurry, shared germs notwithstanding.

Here, unless one is desperately ill, there is drama to be seen all about, and the titanic struggle between life and death is waged every day on the floor, providing the patient with a ringside seat without equal. I would not have exchanged my bed for any other in the hospital. If I had to be ill, this was where I wanted to be, in a room with a view. One morning, while recovering, I stole to the window high above the city to watch the fairy-like dawn creep in from the sea. Two storeys below me I could see into the brightly lit rooms of the luxury annexe housing the solitary wealthy. They were denied the grandeur of my view from the tall old building; I had it all to myself.

There was magic there that Sunday morning. A light blue fog like cigarette smoke wafted over all and gave Dublin a little of the magic of the East. The tall chimneys at Ringsend, vaguely seen, looked like minarets towering over the sleeping city, and a little mackerel cloud hung motionless in a pale, opalescent sky. Too soon a small breeze sprang up, the little cloud took wing, and Dublin, like a dissolute old "shawlie" who had spent too many centuries on a bawdy carouse, staggered into view and brazenly faced another day.

No. . . the things I saw and the people I met are not to be found in the brand-new additions to hospitals. Pity, then, sometimes, the poor rich! So much passes them by.

There Go I. . .

Looking out the hospital window at the end of the storm I shivered. I would soon be discharged and the prospect of going back to my lonely home held no joy. It had held no joy since the missus went away. Me being twelve years older than her, the chances of her dying before me were that much less, but drunken drivers shorten the odds and she had been killed by one while walking on the pavement. So "pretty Kitty" as I used to call her died on me and left me lonely, and that was the only bad thing she ever did on me. They never caught the bastard who killed her either.

I looked idly around the ward at the three companions with whom I had spent the last month. Over in the corner lay old John from Arklow who was on his last legs from booze and chain-smoking. He would never make it out of here I knew. In the other corner lay young John from Bray, who had almost died from bronchial pneumonia, brought on through neglect and heavy drinking and smoking, and no doubt playing the field, the one that is full of birds that say "Goodnight love". On the side opposite these two old Leo lay, having a quiet drag from a cigarette on the sly. He had had a massive heart attack and the Sister in charge, a tall nun, watched him like a hawk. She came in now, a woman of furious energy like the storm outside, and sniffed the air like a pointer.

"You have been smoking again, Mr Quinn," she snapped.

"Only one, Sisther," said Leo.

"Don't you realize that your very existence is put in jeopardy every time you smoke? Is there no way I can stop you from killing yourself?"

"I've been smoking all me life," old Leo growled.

"Do you want to die, Mr Quinn?"

"Sisther, I'd sooner be dead than face the day without a smoke."

"You will, Mr Quinn, you will," promised Sister Maria.

She stood there thinking hard, a dedicated nurse. You were sick, she took over, that was the task God had given her and she worked at it like a Trojan.

"I'll tell you what I'll do, Mr Quinn," she said suddenly coaxing. "I'll have you shifted to my room. I promise I'll come and see you every spare minute I have and we'll talk. Together we can fight your longing for cigarettes, we'll pray and we will win! What do you say?"

"You'd be wasting yer time, Sisther," grunted Leo, "But I thank yeh for the thought."

Defeated she turned to young John. "And how are you today, John. No smoking, I hope."

John, a good-looking man of twenty-six, smiled. "Not one in five weeks, Sister Maria. I'm finished with them."

"Good man," said the nun, smiling for the first time. "Keep it up." She went across to old John's bed and took his pulse while he slept. Finally she turned to me.

"You have been discharged, Mr Redmond," she said coldly. "Please make the necessary arrangements for your clothes to be brought, and don't get back into bed. We have an emergency coming in."

"Suppose I can't reach my friend by phone, supposing he can't bring in my clothes today; what then?"

"You have, Mr Redmond, been discharged."

"Thank Christ for that small mercy anyway," I said, glaring at her. There was no love lost between this good-looking woman and myself. "I'd sooner spend a night in the Park than be here any longer."

Tilting her head scornfully she left the ward. Her hostility towards me was deep-rooted and went back some years to my drinking days. It was here I had been taken after collapsing in the street, and I was blind drunk besides having bronchial pneumonia. The Sister neither understood nor condoned the disease of alcoholism and from that first day had treated me like a drunk, which of course I was then. She treated me with clinical precision, coldly and efficiently, which I resented as only an alcoholic can. It was then a member of Alcoholics Anonymous had visited me and I had decided I needed help. All that was five years ago, a year after the missus died, and I had not touched a drop since. This admission had been for the same complaint, bronchial chest, and I had been unfortunately under the same Sister's care. From the first sight of me she had reacted in exactly the same way as before, and I was too proud to tell her the truth. Nor would I now.

Before heading for the phone I gazed long and hard at the bitter March day I was going out into, and the scene was no bleaker than my thoughts. Across the whitening lawn a vicious wind drove waves of hail at a concrete wall piling a still, frozen breaker against it. My companions of the past month would lie comfortable here tonight while I. . . the thought of that cold, empty house congealed the blood of my heart. Despite all, I would miss the companionship of the hospital. You wouldn't do this to a dog, I told myself, and that bitch of a nun knew full well that I lived alone, that I had been quite ill, that she could well have me back on her hands going out on such a day. March had been a sunny month until today's storm, tomorrow could well bring sunshine again in this freakish spring, there was plenty of room in the large ward for another bed; but this bitch had made up her mind, years ago.

I headed for the phone, raging, in this the winter of my discontent that had lasted six years. Jack, the friend I rang, told me he could not bring in my clothes until after six that night; he might be working overtime and it could be later.

"Jesus," I swore, and headed back for the ward. Both doors of the ward were opened up behind me and wheeled in on a stretcher came a young boy. He was conscious but obviously sedated. He was in terrible shape and gazed dully at me from two black eyes. His forehead was one huge bruise and his face was scratched as if he had been thrown into a blackberry bush, as indeed, I found out, he had.

"What happened to him, Nurse?" I asked the young probationer.

"Hit and run job," she said, "on a country road. He was left to die in a ditch!"

"Jesus Christ," I said, "is there no end to the bloody cruelty of this world?"

The probationer said nothing, but looked shocked, and helped by two others the boy was made comfortable in my bed. He had been in surgery since eight o'clock until now, three hours later, after lying all night in a ditch. The itinerant breed were tenacious of life, I thought. They had to be to survive in this Christian country.

"Will you be with us for lunch, Larry?" said a domestic popping her head in.

"It looks like it, Vera," I said grimly, "and for tea as well."

I felt like a fool standing around in pyjamas, deprived of my island refuge, the bed. I went over and looked at the boy. He appeared to be asleep but felt my presence and opened his eyes.

"Hello," I said, "How are you?"

"Still alive anyway," he mumbled, and I caught a strong, coarse Wexford accent. "I heard the Dochtor say I wasn't too bad."

Maybe, I thought, but he sure looked it. "What happened, son?"

"I heard this car coming at a desperate lick," he said, "An' I up on the bank at the side of the road. . . He must have meant teh get me because he follyed me up the bank and knocked me over inteh the ditch. The Guards said they'd get him."

He closed his eyes then and I left him to take the lunch that was brought in. All that afternoon I wandered around the hospital, and when teatime came my clothes had still not arrived. After tea I took refuge in the television room, and seven o'clock came with its hospital visitors. A couple I knew from Bray spotted me and came in for a chat. They were picking up their son, they told me, and wished me well. Just after that my mortal enemy Sister Maria came in. She gazed at me with ill-concealed hostility.

"Do you intend to leave the hospital tonight, Mr Redmond?" she asked icily.

"I do," I snarled. "But I can't manufacture clothes, can

I? Maybe you'd like me to go out in the snow like this?"

Again I got the disdainful toss of the head and, by Jesus, I swore, I'm taking no more of this. I'd go home with the couple from Bray, clothes or no clothes. They were only too glad to take me and in the time I had left I went back to my old ward to bid them goodbye. I spoke to Leo last, for he lived near me.

"I'll miss yeh, Larry," he said. "Still, though, I'll be out meself in another week."

"I know that, Leo, but now will you listen to me? Will you promise me you'll give up the fags? You'll kill yourself!"

"Aw, for Jesus sake, don't yew start," said Leo angrily. "Don't yew start too. I've enough on my plate with that bloody Sisther!"

"The Sister is right. Why don't you give her and yourself a chance?"

"I'm down teh ten a day. . . de yeh want me teh quit altogether?"

"Yes!"

"I couldn't, Larry. I'd sooner be dead."

"You will be," I promised him. "I'll give you two weeks, Leo, if you don't stop. I know you, when you get home nobody will stop you, you'll smoke all you like."

"I won't. The missus'll be watchin' me."

"Don't make me laugh," I said. "When you're at home you're the Godfather: Marlon Brando has nothing on you!"

"Anyway," he said unexpectedly, "Don't fall out with me, Larry." We shook hands and I went over to the boy's bed and sat down on the chair beside it. He had no visitors.

"When will your Mam and Dad be coming to see you," I asked him.

"I don't know," he said. "Yeh see, I belong teh the travelin' people. Maybe tomorra."

"Tell you what," I said, "Since you're in my bed I'll come in and see you. How about that?"

"Aye," he said doubtfully, "Maybe. . ."

"I'll bring you in comics – can you read?"

"A bit."

"Good, and sweets as well. You'd like that, wouldn't you?"

"Yis, mister."

"What's your name, son?"

"Pather Maher."

"How old are you?"

"Nine. . . ten next birthday."

"Not too old to listen to fairy tales, I hope," I said, "For I've a lot I can tell you."

He smiled. Then my gorge rose. I was suddenly filled with an insane rage, a mad anger, for his smile revealed the broken remains of a once beautiful set of teeth, and I swore to myself that day that if the man who was responsible for this ever crossed my path and I found out I would kill him. It was a stupid vow, but it was born of pity and compassion for the boy.

"I love fairy tales," he told me.

The couple from Bray came then to collect me. "Not ready yet, Larry?" Tom asked.

"I am; I'm going the way I am. I'm through with this bloody hospital and its bloody vicious nuns. . . Come on."

"Jesus Christ," said Tom, "But you're known for a stubborn man."

"So I am, Tom, but come on anyway."

In the corridor I passed Sister Maria without a glance. She stood there staring while I pushed open the door and marched across the snow in my slippers. Tom ran on ahead and had the car door open for me, and as we crunched across the white car park I saw Sister Maria staring through the glass door.

And so, in my pyjamas and dressing gown I came back to my ice-cold house and my ice-cold life. Because I did not give a damn I seemed to be immune to colds and never got even a sniffle from my crazy act of rebellion. And spring was back the next day with a vengeance to help my recovery.

In the weeks that followed I made a small oasis in a twenty-four hour desert by going to see the boy Pather. He came on apace and I liked to think I had a big hand in that. I told him crazy stories about a land of my own invention, Slumberlee, where a marzipan road led through a sugar stick wood where wine-gum vines climbed the trees and lollipop bushes grew in their shade. Where an ice cream mountain melted in the bright sun and sent a torrent crashing down on to Glacier Mint rocks, and a river of lemonade with chocolate banks ran swiftly under a clear sky with an odd candy floss cloud above. I told him of a trembling licorice stick bridge that spanned a dreadful chewing gum swamp and a horrible witch who lived there called "Oul' Instant Whip", who naturally wore gumboots and ploughed her way over to the victims who fell off the bridge and got stuck. The way she turned them into powder and, when she was in a dirty mood, mixed the powder with water, and turned them into anything nasty she felt like – instantly!

I can still hear his laughter.

And then one day I came, and he had gone. I stood beside the empty bed, shattered. There had been no indication the day before that he would be discharged, and the other beds were now occupied by strangers. My old mates were gone and with the boy went my oasis. Sister Maria came in then and gently told me. Tears came to her eyes as she looked at my stricken face. Dimly I heard her. . . it had something to do with a blood clot on the brain, a sudden stroke or something. I stumbled out of the ward blinded by tears.

In the corridor as I wept beside a window the tall, good-looking Sister Maria, who was not my friend, took me gently by the arm. "Come, Mr Redmond," she said softly, "A cup of tea will do you good."

In the staff room, while she poured the tea, she looked with downcast eyes at the cups, lost in thought. Finally she handed me the tea and looked directly at me.

"You know, Mr Redmond, I have been less than kind to you," she said slowly. "I know the dear Lord will forgive my lapse, and I am praying that you will forgive me too. . . Will you? I have come to realize that there is much kindness in you besides being. . ." Her voice trailed off and her face became flushed.

"Besides being a drunk, isn't that it, Sister?"

"I'm afraid it is. I'm sorry."

"And you spotted me five years ago, didn't you?"

"Yes. You had a bad chest all right, but I knew where it came from. Pubs full of smoke."

"And you were right then, Sister, but not this time around. It's five years since I had my last drink. I joined AA after I left here."

"May God forgive me, I didn't know."

"Of course not, Sister, how could you? But being an alcoholic is a killer disease. Did you not know that alcoholism is a disease?"

"No, I regarded it as a vice of a weak person."

"It's a vice all right, but it doesn't necessarily belong to weak people. It respects no single class either: it cuts right across the board – doctors, lawyers, labourers; you name it, AA has them.

"Indeed. Please go on."

"Priests too, did you know that?"

"Yes, well, of course we all know a priest or two who is fond of a little drop."

"Oh yes, Sister, of course a priest is not a dirty, contemptible drunk like me; he's just fond of a little drop. I'm fond of a little drop too."

Sister Maria's colour heightened and I could see she was having difficulty restraining her temper. I decided to try her restraint a little more. This woman had given me a bad time.

"Nuns too, Sister Maria, plenty of them, hospitalized on the quiet; did you know that?"

"What!"

"Yes, Sister, and you can check me out if you like. They

get fond of altar wine, the ones who look after priests and chapels." There was a long pause while we both sipped our tea.

"I can see," said Sister Maria slowly, "that I have quite a bit to learn about alcoholism. I'll make a start, Mr Redmond, I promise you."

"I sincerely hope so, Sister, for it is my opinion that nobody should be unleashed on any hospital without a rudimentary understanding of this century's biggest killer."

"Unleashed," she said quietly. "So I am not forgiven?"

"Well," I said standing up and smiling, "you are forgiven, but only if you do as you said you would and study alcoholism. You'll find a lot of good in alcoholics, perhaps a little more compassion in them than others. You may even be granted the privilege of being able to help one."

"I'll be trying to help from now on."

"OK, Sister, you do that. And I'll help the fella who killed the boy if ever I find him; I'll help him to meet his maker, Sister."

In the weeks that followed summer came in in a rush. I was well again and took to walking Bray Head, up through the magic of a beech wood with its first ethereal leaves that seemed to melt against the blue sky, all the way to the tall concrete cross on top, and along the old carriageway that rumour said had been built against a visit by the old famine Queen, Victoria Regina, to descend near Windgates and so back to Bray.

You have to be fit for a walk like that, and it helps if you don't smoke. One day, looking out over the Irish Sea I sat down on a boulder in the heather to rest. A mile away the horizon was black, shot by lurid lightning flashes, and the distant rumble of thunder came to my ears. Get back, and quickly, I thought. Get off the top of the Head and run for the wood where there would be some shelter, for the storm was coming fast. Hurrying back along the old scenic drive I spotted a man standing in the rising gale at a spot where the old retaining wall had collapsed and there was a thousand feet drop to the sea. He was staggering along, a bottle clutched in his hand. He raised the bottle as I came near, leaning backwards over the precipice; the next gust of wind could take him to his death. I came alongside him running and grabbed him, and we both fell into the heather, but he held on to the whiskey and never spilled a drop.

"We'll have to get to the wood," I shouted above the gale. "Come on, now; I'll give you a hand."

Together we staggered back on to the carriageway. Down below the white horses charged in from the sea, jumping the rocks in a fury of spray. The gulls no longer drifted and wheeled, having fled inland. There was a flash of lightning and a tremendous roll of thunder shook the hill.

"That's where I'd be," he shouted, pointing downwards, "if you had minded your own business."

"Come on, old son," I shouted back. "For Christ's sake come on."

Glaring wildly, he resisted me, finished off the whiskey in a great gulp, and hurled the bottle far out into the wind; we watched it as it bounced off grass tussocks, miraculously missing the rocks until it disappeared from view. I was holding grimly on to his jacket when he twisted around and grabbed me. He was very drunk, red eyes glaring, his long flaxen hair flattened by the wind. He looked like the wrath of God.

"Do you know what I've done?" he screamed. "Do you? Do you!"

"No," I shouted. "And I don't care. Let me go, you mad bastard." And I punched him, hard, in the solar plexus and left him kneeling on the cliff top. He was too big for me to handle, too young, too drunk. If he wanted to kill himself, let him. I had done my best.

I made the beech wood just before the rain struck the tree tops and collapsed into the shelter of a moss-hung rocky outcrop. A couple of minutes later the young drunk came panting in; he lay there beside me gasping, him and his drunken, tortured face and his flattened wheat-field of a head of hair, and I would have been glad never to have seen him again. But here in the shelter of the rock it was at least comparatively quiet, the summer storm far above rushing past.

"Have you got a cigarette?" he asked. "Until I get to a shop."

"No, I had to give them up. But a cigar might help: I carry them in case the longing gets too much."

"Thanks," he said and lit it with shaking hands. "I'm a right mess."

"You are, all right," I agreed. He was unshaven and filthy after what seemed to have been a marathon binge. "You must be, to get yourself into this condition. How long are you on the booze?"

"About a week, I think. I slept in the heather all night."

"How long is it since you had something to eat?"

"I don't know. I think I had a sandwich yesterday, or the day before." He had, under a Wexford brogue, an educated accent. Despite the drunkenness his speech was good.

"How the hell did you come to be on top of the Head anyway?"

"Damned if I know. I must have been in a blackout."

"Well, whatever is troubling you, the booze won't make it any better."

"Jesus Christ, it helps me to forget."

"It must be something terrible you have done altogether."

"Only me and a tinker know just how terrible."

I would have left him and run for it then but for the storm. I had a premonition that he was going to confide in me something that I did not want to hear. I had enough troubles of my own, with the loneliness and the drink and trying to give up cigarettes.

"I ran over a young boy in Wexford a few weeks ago, and I drove on. Jesus Christ, how could I do a thing like that!"

"Was the young boy from Gorey?" I asked.

"In a way. He came from a tinker family who were just outside the town."

"Was he badly hurt?"

"He's dead; died in Loughlinstown Hospital last week, just when I thought everything would be all right."

And so here was the man I had sworn to kill if ever we met. Here he was beside me and I had probably saved his life! So much for my foolish Walter Mitty mind, for in the face of such distress I could not find it in my heart even to dislike him.

"Just when you thought you were off the hook," I said bitterly.

He looked hard at me, leaned away and started to vomit, a dry tearing retching that brought back the past to me. Presently the paroxysm passed and he sat up again. His face was streaming sweat and he looked desperately ill.

"If you want to put it that way," he said, "but I've paid for it since, oh my Jesus have I paid. I've nearly lost my reason; I'm nearly losing it now."

Overhead the worst of the storm has passed and soon I would be able to travel again.

"I suppose you were drunk behind the wheel?"

"Yes."

"I could find it in my heart to pity you if you had not driven on. Why didn't you stop?"

"That's what I can't forgive myself for. . . I froze to the wheel, I went on and on; it was like going down a tunnel with no end and no turning. I don't know how long it lasted but when I did turn back the boy had been picked up. It all happened so fast: one minute an empty lane, the next the boy in the headlights. . . I just barely brushed him with the mudguard. . ."

"You did it at speed," I told him, "and he landed on a rock with his head; that's what killed him."

He looked hard at me, and since his fit of vomiting he was sobering rapidly. "How come you know so much about it?" he asked.

"He came into hospital the day I was discharged; as a matter of fact they put him in my bed; that's how I know." There was a long silence.

"So you met him then," he said at last.

"I *knew* him," I said vehemently. "I used to go to the hospital and tell him fairy stories. He was coming on great and then. . . the blood clot. . . the poor little devil."

"Christ, you must hate me!"

"I'm trying to but I can't. I do pity you, though. You're the one who has to live with it."

"I'm the one, all right," he said grimly. "Me, Stephen Hogan from Gorey!"

And suddenly I was filled with fury. "What did you want to tell me your name for? Sure, I didn't want to know it, or you, or be dragged into your troubles."

"It'll ease your conscience, won't it? You can turn me over to the police, can't you?"

"And five years in jail will ease yours, is that it? Well, you can live on in your own hell. I won't bail you out."

I sat there thinking long thoughts. Sure, I could get him jailed, but was this young man beside me to be broken on the wheel of life for one mistake? What good would it do to report the matter to the police? It wouldn't bring my little friend back, and paying his debt to society would alter nothing. The general public would grunt their satisfaction that justice had been done and turn to the sports page. As regards the moral aspect of the thing, I was in no position to criticize anyone. After the missus went I had been a mobile menace until the Gardai relieved me of my license and saved me from killing someone. I glanced at the young man beside me, at his careworn face and trembling hands and, Christ help me, I thought, there but for the grace of God go I! Jail or no jail, this man would pay for many a long day. I lit a cigar for myself and gave him another one. The storm was over and now the sun burst through the trees, dappling the floor of the small forest. The forbidden nicotine was balm to my soul.

"What do you do for a living?" I asked idly.

"I'm a farmer," he said, "and a good one. I've three hundred acres of the best land in Ireland."

"So you're rich then?"

"I suppose so."

"You're young to inherit so big a farm."

"I come from a big family," he said. "In the business way, I mean: hotels, auctioneering, big people in Wexford."

"Well, don't worry," I said, "I won't tell the Guards. You'll have to do that yourself."

"It'll kill the father and mother!"

"Well then don't do it. You could, if you wanted to, make restitution to the tinker boy's family."

"How? I'd give them any amount they wanted."

"Would they drink it, do you think?"

"I think so. . . in fact I'm sure, the father's a hard man for the booze."

"Well then, try it another way. You could cut a piece off your farm and build a lay-by for the travelling people, and do the job right, properly surfaced and serviced with a couple of tigeens for a start. You have a whole lifetime to make restitution to young Pather's kin, and you could try from today to give up the drink. I could show you the way."

"How?"

"Join Alcoholics Anonymous and find out."

"I've been in it over two years," came the surprising answer.

"It's just that I had a slip. . . I thought I could drink normally. I'm mad enough for anything."

"Aren't we all," I said quietly, "when we take a drink."

"I'd need a bit of professional advice to get the tinker lay-by started."

"You've got it now," I told him; "I'm a builder, retired."

"And you'd come down with me? It would take a while. What about your wife. . . I mean, are you married?"

"She died a few years ago."

"I'm sorry," he said. And that made two of us, but whatever small future lay before me she would be glad for me this day. "God bless you for what you have done for me!" And that was another good statement, that I had helped him, for the reverse was the case. For the first time in years a day had passed like a flash, a day totally involved in another's troubles, a day in which self-pity had gone out the door. I was rejoining the human race.

I rose, a bit stiffly for it was autumn for me, season of mists and mellow fruitfulness. "What are you going to do now, Stephen?" I asked him as we went slowly down the road towards Bray.

He smiled weakly. "Get on the Wexford bus, I suppose, and get back home."

"In your condition? I wouldn't recommend it!"

"And what would you propose instead?"

"That you spend a few days with me, God knows I've plenty of room. You can phone your people from my place, but try looking like your mother's son before you go home."

"OK," he said, "I'll do that. Will you come back to Wexford with me?"

"Yes. We'll get right into the lay-by thing. But first it's a few good feeds and a few AA meetings for you, Wicklow style."

He stumbled then and came to a halt. "I need a doctor, I think," he said.

"I *know* you need a doctor," I answered, "and I'll get you one as soon as we get home. He's an alcoholic himself. You'll be in good hands."

After a short rest we resumed our journey. We had almost reached my house when the cardiac ambulance from Loughlinstown swept past, its siren shrieking.

"Who's in the ambulance?" I asked a friend on the pavement. "Do you know?"

"I do know," he said forcefully. "That's your old hospital mate Leo, the one you told to stop smokin'. I don't know what all the rush is about: he was dead comin' out o' the house."

Leo dead: and two weeks to the day, as I had predicted. I shivered. Someone had walked over my grave.

"A gas thing," said the neighbour, "Leo was made a great grandfather this mornin'. Funny oul' life, isn't it?"

"It is," I said, "a very funny old life." And quietly, with my young companion, I walked back into it.

5

CHANGING PLACES

A Desert Place

I had cleaned and oiled my old .22 until it shone. It was twelve years since we had gone hunting together, twelve years since I had pulled a trigger in Ireland, twelve years in which I had dreamed of this moment.

The beech wood halfway up the mountain was all around me, and through the scattered holly bushes on the edge I could see the bright glare of sunshine on frosted white grass. In the distance the sea, blue as in summer, sparkled away to a hazy shadow that was Howth Hill on the far side of the bay. The air was like wine and my breath went before me in little clouds as I sauntered uphill through the dead leaves of the lost years. I was not expecting sport here. A mile further up where the trees gave way to holly, and the holly then to furze, was where I was expecting my first shot.

It was January; it would be hot as hell in the north-west of Western Australia, where a rusty mountain of iron ore in a red desert spilled its dust and guts and wealth, to create havoc around the world. I had survived to escape. There were plenty who would not.

I went on softly through the wood, and the past kept easy pace with me. Happiness I held now in the palm of my hand and, savouring the moment, I thought back to the unhappiness. I remembered how it had been in the false dawn with the stars still overhead, bright satellites streaming across the clear sky; I remembered heading towards the dining hall in fear, knowing that in an hour the sun would leap over the horizon and I would have to face another murderous onslaught for another ten hours. To remember the gathering heat of the morning, the persecution of the bush flies, mad for water, drinking my sweat. And then the dreaded afternoon shift when the kangaroos sought shade, when the desert lizards crawled under a rock, and even the bush flies hid from the sun; working with reddened eyes from salt sweat and iron ore dust, when to save my sanity I would work mechanically, dreaming of a land where there were no deserts, where the trees grew tall and the grass green, where brown rivers tumbled from mountain bogs, and the sun held no terror. And, waking from dreams, I would wipe the sweat from my eyes and look in hate at the ugly raddle-faced whore of a country that was trying to kill me.

"You won't," I'd snarl as I staggered over to the water-bag and washed a couple of salt tablets down. I'd work away until six, with a waterfall crashing through my mind and the merciless sun, lord of all the dust and dry rivers and slaughtered vegetation, would give me another beating, but he would lose. . . for that day anyway. For I would hide in my special refuge, dreaming of a trout-rod and a .22, old friends still safe in my sister's house in Dublin, and for one more day I would survive.

It was good now to remember the terrible day when the sun had robbed the bubble from my spirit level, one hundred and twenty degrees in the shade – though there was no shade where I was; to remember poor Basilio who had collapsed an hour later and had been flown to hospital in Perth that night. Gasping, we had met at the water-bag: a big, tough Sicilian and a small Dubliner.

"Mamma mio," he panted, "It ees a hot."

"It is, Baz', me oul' flower," I gasped, "But at least you're more used to it than me. You can take it better."

"No," he said, "Nobody can a take a that."

He pointed at the sun and looked at me, tears of exhaustion in the spaniel-brown eyes and said with feeling, "Every day that bloody bastardo up there. . . he beata my bloody brains out."

Soon after, they took him away. Here, safe in the wood I could afford to remember how it had been with me, a man outside his own God-given environment who could neither adjust nor accept but could only labour like a brute in order to get the fare back to where he had come from.

Well up the mountain now, clear of the trees and with the holly giving way to furze, a breathtaking view was unfolding, but I could not see it, for I was too far away in a red desert. From miles off, carried on the thin wind, came the sound of a hunting horn and the yodelling music of a pack of hounds. Two hen pheasants rose from under my feet and with a whir and a clatter of wings brought me back to Ireland.

On the opposite mountain a gleam through the trees showed the river where I had caught my first trout last autumn when I had arrived back home. The sheer joy had impelled me, no longer young, up the side of a mountain like a wild goat to a well-remembered pool. The first cast. . . the strike. . . the fight of a good fish for his life; in the end I grassed him, and eleven others after him.

That evening in the pub in Enniskerry, when I should have been garrulous on a couple of pints and a "large one", I had been strangely quiet. With twelve trout in the bag I should have come down from the mountain ten feet tall, like Cuchulain. I should have gone into the pub and brought the summer with me. But two hours before closing time I had left, not even having being warned for singing.

A cloud had seemed to have fallen over me. Even on the bus, homeward bound, the mood had hung around like a bad smell and long before I had come to the GPO in Dublin, I had been back again, jug of beer in hand, under the shadow of the iron hill – Mount Tom Price, Western Australia.

To watch the lurid glow from behind the red hill as the sun went down was to know fear, for this was the way it must have been when the world was young, when the first intelligent biped stood up, sniffed the breeze and shivered. The hot wind, searing over a thousand miles, a million dead mallee bushes, through a billion petrified twigs and branches, had a sibilant whisper that would put the fear of God into an unfrocked priest. An ignorant peasant from the back-blocks of Yugoslavia, an unlettered brute from Crete, a drunken mad Jew who had escaped the gas chamber, all could feel this. Put an animal here and it would be fearful, for this place was out to kill you. Even if you quit in time, as I had, it was still too late; you would never be the same again. You would carry the scars to your grave.

But to hell with spoiling a glorious morning with sour thoughts and God's goodness with bitter memories, for surely what I was looking at, walking on, gazing over was God's handiwork. In the place where I had come from if you could see God's work at all, it was cruel work. If, I often said to myself, He had taken seven days to make the world He must have made this joint on the eighth day, slapped it together on a Monday morning after a dirty weekend, and with no pay coming from the job threw stones at it, for the desert floor was littered with rocks as far as the eye could see.

Helping Father Quinlan, the travelling priest of the mining camps, to set up his altar one Sunday morning on top of the juke box in the recreation room, I had said this to him for devilment, to see how he would react. He had burst out laughing and shaken his head.

"It would take more than that to shock me," he had said. "You Irish, you're all talk."

"Yes," I had said, suddenly serious, "But tell me, can you see the hand of God in this?" In weary distaste I pointed out the window to a land that seemed to be lit up with magnesium flares. It was still only ten a.m., the day was young, but already the heat was intolerable. The sun bounced back off the rocks, each rock with a sparkling focal point like a magnifying glass. High up on Mount Tom Price a pink wind blew from where the ant-like mechanical diggers were gouging out the iron ore, Sunday morning or no Sunday morning, God notwithstanding.

"Can you see His hand there?" I pointed at the rusty mountain.

"Yes," said Fr Quinlan, "I see His hand everywhere."

"Maybe I do too," I said bitterly.

"Not your way, though," he said quietly. "You ask too many questions. You are too complicated for a simple priest."

He stood before me in khaki shorts and shirt, as sun-bronzed as myself, a young man doing a hard job in a hard country, and with a sudden flash of intuition I realized that the hardest part of his job was not the hundreds of miles he travelled from one mining camp to another, taking his life in his hands in a Land-Rover with two spare wheels, a couple of cans of beans and a water-bag. He had no fear of the desert that frightened me. I was the desert that terrified him.

"You're no simple priest," I said stubbornly. "You've been around the world. You played cricket for Australia. You've seen the poverty of Calcutta and the wealth of London. You've been around, Father Quinlan, you've travelled."

"If I had never travelled further than from here to there," he replied quietly pointing towards the iron mountain, "I would still have come further than you. Look within yourself, Irish. That's the only answer I can give you."

And now, with the last of the tall trees behind me I slipped the safety-catch off the rifle and moved through the bushes silently. Now we would see, find out in the moment of truth if the sight, the fingers, the reflexes had dimmed with the years. Nothing stirred as I left the bushes and came to a field between two woods, but there was my target: on a rock, pointing into the breeze, sat a fox, tongue lolling out after a hard run, staring back towards the distant sound of the hounds. They would never get him now, but I would!

I slid the rifle noiselessly on to a fence post and got him dead in the sights. And then it came to me. This was an Irish fox I was about to shoot. For him it was still penal days with every hand raised against him. When myxomatosis had killed off the rabbits he had faced into a famine as brutal as ever my ancestors had faced, he with no meat, us with no spuds, but the pair of us still surviving. Here! Perhaps if statistics were available it would be found that half his race had died too, unseen and unwanted in their little mud houses beneath the ground, as mine had died in their mud cabins above ground.

I watched him, and he was laughing mistily in the frosty air, sitting on the rock, and the two of us looking over the gentle majesty of half the County Wicklow. Is this, asked my mind, what you came back all this way to do? To murder an Irish fox, the survivor of another Irish famine? And in sudden revulsion I took my .22 by the front sight, dashed the stock off the fence post and broke the rifle in half.

The fox jumped as if I had shot him and, tail streaming, tore across the white grass to the safety of the opposite wood.

I could have been killed by my impulsive action, but now I threw the magazine into a dense clump of blackberry bushes, ejected the bullet from the breech and battered my old friend to death on the rock.

I had had a wall of steel across my mind for years, but time and suffering had taken great lumps out of it as surely as the mechanical diggers were gouging away the iron mountain in Western Australia. I had not learned much, but a little was a start. Somewhere inside me there was elation, mixed with unspeakable regret. My hunting days were all over, I had fired my last shot, caught my last trout. Never. . . ever. . . again! My own struggle for existence had been too bitter.

Sighing, I found my penknife, cut down an ash plant with a good handle, and walked back inoffensively through the wood.

The Dead Rivers Of Dublin

Just across the Liffey, at the bottom of Winetavern Street, there used to be a fishing tackle shop called Keegan's; gone now, alas, with most of the rivers that gave it its trade. In a glass case in the window there was a magnificent seven and a half pound brown trout that had been caught in the River Camac, at some far away place called Clondalkin. I was bitten early by the fishing bug, and the first real day of spring saw the urge to go fishing rise in me as irresistibly as the tide that brought the salmon up the Liffey.

In my memory my friend Colin seems always to have been with me, for we were two of a kind. We loved to go rambling in green fields, and there was an estate just outside Crumlin village where we scaled the stone wall and lived on beechmast, walnuts and late blackberries for the day, returning home laden with plunder, pockets full of wheat gleaned from the golden stubble which we chewed surreptitiously in school. It was Colin who first showed me the trick of catching perch with tadpoles. They swarmed beside the quarry and they were easier to get than digging worms. If there was an easy way of doing something my pal would find it. He was that kind of boy, easy-going, thoughtful, given to much reading like myself. Together we roamed the Coral Island with Ralph and Peterkin and wished we could exchange the quarry for the dangers of the lagoon. The fact that nearly every year the quarry claimed a boy was lost on us, for we were among the last of our age group to learn to swim. Anything that smacked of serious athletic effort was avoided by us both. Soccer, Gaelic football and even hurling were anathema to us, and when Dolphin's football ground was packed with fans we would be quietly watching a cork as the roar of the crowd came faintly on the breeze.

We learned things the other boys knew nothing about. We knew that swans mated for life, and that if one died the other pined away of a broken heart. We saw the parent swans drive the young ones off, scattering the family to the four winds. After all, there would be another mating in the spring and the quarry's food supply was limited. So, the youngsters had to fend for themselves, the inexorable law of nature. The same law operated in the overcrowded Liberties, though we did not perceive that! We did not notice that in some struggling families the mother steeled her heart as, on reaching sixteen, each of her brood quietly disappeared, one by one, to join some relative abroad who had blazed the trail.

My boyhood summers passed pleasantly enough thanks to the quarry and the canals. When I was about eleven my favourite uncle started to drop by our house for a rest and a cup of tea. He lived on the north side and somebody had told him about a river off the Naas Road at Clondalkin, a long bike ride. The best river in Ireland, my uncle said, and he always had a bag of trout to prove it. They were delicious and beautiful and I went mad to catch one. But I had to wait a couple of weary seasons before I could go with him. I was a runt, too small to ride my father's bike, and with no money for a proper rod either I had to wait and fret. But at thirteen I got a job after school exercising greyhounds and slowly scraped up the money to really go fishing. Hooks were a penny each, catgut was expensive too and the rod twelve shillings – a fortune! However, the day came when by lowering the saddle I could manage my father's bike, and together my uncle and I set out and reached the lovely little river.

I was trembling with excitement as he put up his rod. I had been forbidden to put up mine until he had shown me the rudiments of clear-water worm fishing. It was a skilful game played at close quarters to the shy trout; one crept along the bank, keeping out of sight, dropping the worm above the fish so that it passed them at exactly the same speed as the water. He started angling and after fifteen minutes turned a puzzled face to me.

"Not a bite," he said and started to fish another pool. At the end of an hour he placed his rod on the bank.

"Not a nibble," he said quietly. "There's something wrong here."

Making no attempt to hide we walked to the edge of the river. There was indeed something wrong. The bottom of the pool was speckled with the white bellies of trout, many of them quite large. My uncle had caught a six-pounder on this river, but he would never again catch another fish here and it was my destiny to arrive the day after the Camac died. That was the day after the paper mill opened. For this river was not slowly poisoned but died at a stroke, and such were the times that not a voice was raised in protest. There were plenty more rivers, then. Even my heartbroken uncle agreed that jobs were more important than trout, but I never did. My heart cried out against the outrage, and cried out again when I saw the rest of the natural heritage of the Dubliner destroyed by pollution: the Tolka, the Knocksedan, the Poddle's upper reaches; all the canals silted up and the quarries filled with Dublin's dirt.

The last river left, the Dodder, is now under threat, and I'm told people on the north side are fighting to restore the Tolka and the Royal Canal. But it is much easier to kill a river than to revive it, though if the will of the English people can restore the Thames after it had been polluted for a century then anything can be done. It only waits for the day when the people of Dublin will rise up in anger and demand, industry notwithstanding, that their birthright be restored to them. I may yet catch a trout on the Camac, though my time is running short. I do not, fortunately, go on for ever, but the river does.

The Gladiator

Jim Stephens gazed up at the half-completed multi-storey building and gave a sigh of utter weariness. He was a stocky man in his early fifties, and last week he had dyed his hair. His wife said it made him look ten years younger; he wished he had felt it.

They were looking for carpenters and here he was again, the ageing gladiator in the bloody arena. He gazed around looking for the head that carried the yellow plastic helmet; red for the workers, white for the leading hands, yellow for the general foreman. Some young fellow half his age would be wearing it. . . some young smart alec. Just lately they seemed to be jumping out of holes in the ground. Tight-faced, tough, merciless young men: shove over, Daddio. . . on your way, Grandad. . . grab this, old timer. . . Smart, too, in the new methods of construction, but not a carpenter, a real one, in a dozen of them. What the hell had happened to the building game since the last war, anyway?

He spotted the foreman eventually. He was standing on the scaffold about sixty feet up. It was the place, Jim knew, that he had deliberately chosen to interview men looking for work; if you hadn't the head for heights you wouldn't look for a job here. Another smart alec, another clean-limbed young genius who was on his way up, to where? He'd find out all right! Give him another thirty years in this racket and he'd find out, by Jesus he'd find out; that is, if he lasted that long.

Jim started briskly up the ladder. He was lucky in a way: Old Man Time had not yet destroyed his head for heights, like all his old mates. He never met any of them on the building sites nowadays. Where had they all gone? On the scrap heap, he thought bitterly, ousted from the game by failing nerve, eyes that had grown less sharp and legs that had become too tired to climb. Gone, like the ornate cornices, moulded skirtings and four-panel doors. Gone, all gone. And he was one of the last left, still battling for a crust in the dusty arena.

The ladder as he came half way up yawed sickeningly, and this was what the cur on top was watching: if he slowed down now his chance of a job was gone. He kept going, never faltering, and reached the scaffold on top in creditable time. He drew deep breaths as he came near the foreman to avoid panting or showing too much sign of strain. He grinned confidently as he stepped onto the scaffold.

"Mornin'," he said easily, "'ear yer lookin' fer chippies."

The young foreman slowly appraised him, missing nothing. Jim gazed back, observing the tall, thin, figure, good-looking in a tight-faced way, cold blue eyes looking out from under the plastic helmet, expressionless. Were they mass-producing this type now? All out of the same tight-lipped stable; Jesus Christ, had they forgotten how to smile?

"Yeah," he drawled. "You used to this kind o' work?"

"Yeah."

"Got ter move quick an' lively on this site, mate."

"I'm still worth me porridge."

"Got yer tools wit' yer?"

"In the boot of me bomb!"

"OK then. Start at the top. Russell is the leadin' hand. I'll get yer particulars later."

Going down the ladder to collect his tools he wondered how long this job would last for him. And there was a laugh thrown in for good measure. "Collect yer tools." He was starting to wonder why carpenters bothered to carry them anymore. All he needed now to carry them was his two hands. A rule, a pencil, a spanner, a nail bag, and a hammer in his belt, and he took a saw for giggles. From the site office he collected a red helmet that nearly fitted him, and he was ready for work. At the last moment he remembered and exchanged the good hammer he was carrying for the one with the broken claw. He only needed it for bashing anyway, and he was not going to ruin his good one belting steel panels into place.

The long climb to the ninth floor seemed endless. For the first three floors it was easy going, a smooth waterfall of terrazzo steps going up and up, a writhing chrome snake of shining handrail alongside. But after that he entered the unfinished section of the building, the handrail was a flimsy affair of light timber that was useless for easing the climb. As he came near the top it petered out altogether, and he panted along near the wall, on the safe side.

On the last landing he paused, out of sight, to get his breath. Mustn't be too used up when he came on deck; there would be another of the tight-faced brigade there waiting for him. He rested his arms on a windowless opening and gazed out over the sunny city. It lay spread beneath him in the early morning sunshine, a thing of infinite remoteness, a toy city inhabited by ants driving their tiny cars through the streets and parkways apparently without purpose. He wondered at how many trees there were in the city, each back garden with its half dozen fruit trees, the inviolate Adelaide parklands that ringed the packed central city, whose silhouette grew higher every year. From above it looked like a city in a forest.

A light veil of mist, quickly dispersing, gave it a fairylike appearance, and it looked quiet and peaceful and orderly. But, as Caesar two thousand years before had gazed into another arena, Jim knew he was looking down on an area of bloody conflict where ageing gladiators fought on with fading eyes, tired muscles and jaded skills. There were plenty more like him down there.

He turned abruptly and walked the last few steps up and out on to the latest multi-storey building to meet the latest member of the tight-faced brigade. He nearly laughed outright when the leading hand stopped him. This one was stockier, even younger than the foreman, but the cold blue eyes and set mouth were in the pattern.

"Yew the new man?" he asked.

Jim nodded. "Where'll I start?"

"Over there, dad."

And suddenly Jim was seething with rage. He was walking away when the "dad" bit came and stopped him in his tracks.

"Don't flatter yourself, sonny," he said tightly, "I'm not yer fuckin' father."

He was feeling better as he walked on, but the encounter had not enhanced his chances of holding his job. Junior would have his eye on him now! He would have to work that much harder and mistakes, even small ones, were out. "Fuck everything," he thought savagely, "I'm not takin' that kinda talk."

He felt the leading hand's eye on him several times during the morning, but he toiled away bolting the hated steel panels together as the sun rose in the heavens and the concrete floor started to hot up. Already, although it was only a quarter to ten, it was ninety degrees in the shade, and there is no shade on top of a multi-storey building. The sweat streamed off him and the protective plastic helmet he was compelled to wear did not make things any easier. He had always hated to wear a hat and now, at his age, to be made to wear this contraption! The steel panels, thick with grease in order to prevent concrete sticking to them, seemed heavier than ever before, and for the first time in his life the thought shot across his mind that he might not see this day out. Growing old, he thought tiredly, and suddenly he knew that the shadow of the scrap-heap was upon him, that he was almost there. There had to be a day, one day, when Old Man Time gave the thumbs down sign to every gladiator, and maybe this was his day. Jesus Christ. . . he'd sooner be dead, an' then there was the missus, not too strong. . .

At "smoko" the foreman came and took his "particulars".

"Married?"

Yes, he was married. . . yes. . . there was only himself and one dependent. . . yes. . . yes. . . fuck off, buster, and let a man drink his tea in peace.

"We pay 'ere on Thursdays. We'll be 'oldin' two back days."

Yeah. . . yeah. . . and, fuck it, there goes the whistle.

It was time to face the wall of steel again. Jim swore softly and rose stiffly to his feet. Far below the city looked glassy in the heat glare. Six more hours to go! Jim's working mate was a "new Australian", a swarthy thick-set Italian, strong as a bull, but a good bloke, quick with a hand when Jim was struggling.

"Thanks, mate, 'preciate it."

A real mate, even if he did smell a little ripe from chewing garlic, and as the thought came to him Jim's weathered face broke into a smile. The new Australian grinned back. In a country that was hostile to his race he had made a friend. Jim's grin grew wider.

"Work on the windward side o' me, mate," he said. "We'll 'it it off better."

Mates! In the old days every man was your mate. Nowadays they were hard to find, hard to find as a good union man. It was the union that had bound them together in the old days, fighting solidly shoulder to shoulder for what these pups took for granted and treated with contempt. And that was just one other thing that had gone, gone with the picket lines and the poverty, the rallies and the baton charges, the hardship and the grandeur; gone too the vision glorious that had carried them forward irresistibly. . . to this! These faint-hearted, filleted, lack-lustre union men had allowed their real gains to be eroded, until now the capitalist had regained complete control and it was even illegal to strike, palmed off with one-sided state awards!

"Like Australia?" Jim asked his mate.

"Notha like now. Isa too bloody 'ot."

"Yew can say that again, cobber!"

"Isa good country. . . plenty work. . . gooda money. . ." He frowned, trying to express himself in this harsh, strange language. "Alla timea work. . . nobodya sing, adance, nobody isa happy."

"'Ow de yer mean mate?"

"Ina Napoli everybody apoor, but each help each other. You gotta job, you gotta money you alucky, you take your friend for a drink, no? In Australia, nobody acare."

Jim stopped and picked up another panel. It was almost too hot to touch. This was the point where he should step in and pull the Italian into gear. Any of the young tight-lipped brigade would have done it. "If yer don't like it 'ere, Charlie, why don't yer go 'ome, back tew yer own flamin' country!" The parrot cry of every stupid galah in the southern continent. Jim sighed.

"You're right, mate," he agreed.

So the Italian felt it too, the lack of joy, of comradeship, of sharing, of the qualities that had stood for Australia in the good old days when things were bad. Somewhere along the road to better living, arbitration boards and state awards these precious qualities had been lost. To be a good trade unionist now was to be smeared with the tar brush of "communist". They had even invented fancy words for it. "Chronic industrial malcontent" was one of their phrases. Kick up a row about unsafe scaffolding, and that's what you were. That staircase that he had climbed this morning: no guard-rail for three floors, and these men had been climbing it for weeks and had kept their mouths shut. They couldn't afford to be sacked, too much on time payment, furniture, fridges, houses, cars – especially the cars.

The day the employers had been made to make it possible for a worker to own a car had been the day of their greatest victory. Hire purchase and cars: they had sold their independence for a status symbol, a mechanical bauble. Now it was a part of their tool kit, necessary for chasing work and going to work, and the suckers paid for it out of their own pockets!

The whistle went as he was lifting another greasy panel and he simply dropped it where he stood, wiped his hands on a piece of rag, and picked up his lunch box.

"Where we 'ave a lunch, Jeem?"

"On the staircase, mate, out o' this sun. Be a bit of a draught there too."

They joined the crowd making for the comparative cool of the staircase. It was stinking hot. The white glare off the burning concrete floor hurt his eyes, his feet were aching and sticky with sweat. The squad spread out, one on each step. Boots were taken off and the steaming helmets were thankfully laid aside. Now, thought Jim, is the time for idiots to start talking, not about politics or trade unionism or stairs nine storeys up without a protection rail, but about cars, stinking dangerous expensive cars. It soon got going, bits of it drifting to his ears: "She's burnin' too much oil, mate"; "Mine's runnin' 'ot"; "Yer might 'ave a cracked 'ead gasket there"; "Yer, that's what I'm scared of, I'll 'ave a job done on 'er if the overtime keeps up."

"Aw, shurrup about yer bloody cars," Jim snapped. "Can't yer find somethin' else ter mag about?"

"What's eatin' the old timer?" A young fellow further down the stairs asked the question.

"Blowin' a gasket, like Snowy's car," cracked another. They stared at him, grinning but resentful.

"I'm flamin' sick 'earin' about yer cars; how about talkin' about somethin' that counts?"

"Like what, dad?"

"Like a staircase nine floors up without an 'andrail, son!"

There was a sudden silence. Nobody, it seemed, wanted to talk about an open staircase nine floors up. Jim regarded them with contempt.

"I thought not," he said bitterly. "And don't yer want ter know it's against union rules. I don't suppose the half of yer have even got a paid-up union ticket."

"To hell with the union!" It was the first young fellow who had spoken. "They're out o' date. The awards take care of us."

"Oh, do they? And who negotiates with the bosses? You?"

The young carpenter's face flushed but he made no reply. The sneering "old timer" bit was over, and an embarrassed silence hung over the staircase.

"I'll tell yer somethin' fer nothin," Jim said pointedly. "Ye're another renegade who's havin' a free ride on my back. It's payin' the few bob a week that bothers yew, nothin' else!"

"I'm not in the union," a red-faced man in his early thirties spoke up, "an' I'm not goin' ter be in the fuckin' union. That bloke is right, we don't need them any more."

"So. . . another two-bit capitalist 'oo 'as everythin' goin' fer 'im. You get paid fer public 'olidays?"

"We get it pro rata. . . in our wages."

"Then why ain't yer enjoyin' yerself on public 'olidays, instead of bein' on the bones of yer arse? I suppose yer 'ave superannuation and long service leave in yer wage packet too?"

"Long service leave is in our award. Where 'ave yer been all yer life?"

Jim stood up. He was seething with rage. "An' who the 'ell ever qualifies for long service leave?" he shouted. "A few government-employed chippies, that's all. Do yer mean ter tell me that any man 'ere is ever likely ter collect it? What long service? A year, six months at a time is the best yer can expect in this game on any site, if yer lucky – if yer 'oldin yer mouth the right way!"

He shuffled into his boots then, a stocky man, still strong, with the harsh lines that sun and wind and toil had etched indelibly on his face.

"Listen ter me," he said thickly, "I've been in this game for thirty-nine years, thirty-nine bloody rough years. I've built churches, an' schools, and state houses, an' private 'ouses." His voice rose as rage possessed him. "An' shit 'ouses. An' where's my superannuation an' long service leave? Me. . . an' men like me 'ave built this flamin' country, and fought fer it too, an' where is it? Where is it?" he roared. "Answer me, answer me that, you galahs who don't need a union! I'm listenin'!"

In the dead silence that followed the whistle blew piercingly and the men slowly filed out on to the concrete. The dreaded afternoon shift when the mercury forgot to stop climbing was under way, the shift that separated the men from the boys. It was this, coupled with insecurity, that drove them into lesser occupations before they were forty, and the experience of a lifetime was thrown on the scrap-heap.

"You tell them, Jeem," the Italian said excitedly. "My word, Jeem, you tella them plenty." He was grinning with satisfaction, delighted with his new mate. Jim grinned wryly back. From now on he would be a marked man.

"Look around fer a new mate, Amelio," he advised, "I've just talked me way out of a job."

As they went to work on the steel panels concreting began on the wall beside them, an air compressor started up to drive the concrete vibrator, and a few yards away a pneumatic drill went into action. In the fury of sound, in the roar and the dust and the heat the afternoon shift got under way.

Jim climbed stiffly up the wall of steel he had helped to erect; he had a few minor jobs to attend to there. Far below the shimmering landscape baked peacefully under a ferocious sun and he caught a glimpse of a distant river with its attendant guard of tall gum-trees along its banks. Behind him the bedlam of sound was increasing in tempo, and his head was aching. He knew a deep hole on that river where a man could sit with his back to a gum-tree in the lovely shade and catch himself a feed of fish, maybe even a murray cod if he was lucky. And listen to God's tranquil silence. A little puff of wind went past his face and he took off his helmet to let it ruffle his dyed hair. He never even saw the enormous crane hook as it swung towards him. One moment he was dreaming of a river, the next the world exploded in a ball of red fire and he hung perilously over the wall, unconscious, his legs bent at a curious angle, trapped in the steel reinforcing between the panels.

Like another carpenter two thousand years before, they came and took him down from his steel cross. When he came to he was lying on the concrete floor. Amelio was sitting on the concrete cradling his head in his lap and warding off the sun and the flies until the stretcher came.

"Keep steall, Jeem," he said softly. "You no move."

"Am I hurt bad, Amelio?" His head felt as if it would burst, and both his legs ached terribly. His mouth tasted of blood and he became aware that Amelio was holding a handkerchief to his head to try to staunch the flow.

"Crane hook hitta you in the head, then comea back an' hitta you in the legs. Theenk botha legs broken, Jeem. You no move."

Both legs broken and a belt from a quarter-ton crane hook, not bad! This was it, his passport to freedom. As sure as he lay on the ninth floor of Adelaide's latest multistorey building he knew, instinctively, that in six months he would be a whole man again, but he was not going to do it that way. "Play it cool, daddio," that's what the curs had told him today, and that's what he was going to do. He might be on crutches unable to walk, his back might be crooked, he might suffer from blinding headaches, he might even be short a few marbles, a ha'penny short of a shillin' from the head blow, but he had plenty of time to work that out in hospital.

Whatever way he played it, there was going to be a great big fat compensation cheque at the end of this: long service leave, superannuation and pension all rolled into one. He moaned softly as the storm of sound reached a crescendo.

"My head, Amelio," he said. "It's burstin'. . . Make them

stop."

"Stopa the noise!" the Italian screamed. "Makea them stop." As the noise died down Jim saw that it was the young foreman Amelio had screamed at. Jim's leading hand, Junior, was with him.

"It wouldn't 'a been so bad if 'e'd been wearin' his 'elmet. He was told it was a condition of employment, wasn't 'e?"

The foreman nodded. "He was told. . . an' 'e was wearin' it, just before he was struck." He turned to the Italian. "That's right, ain't it, Amelio?"

"Thatsa right!" Amelio was grinning.

"But I saw. . ." Junior protested.

"You saw nothin'! I've just told you what you saw," the foreman said flatly. He took Amelio's helmet off his head and walked behind a pile of steel panels; when he came back there was a gaping hole in the helmet. He placed it gently under Jim's head as the ambulance men, carrying a stretcher, came out on to the ninth floor.

Seventy Feet Below

As the Roaring Twenties came to a close the death knell of Dublin's Liberties district sounded. Few heard the bell, but to me it came loud and clear. I had no idea of the vast projected slum clearances. All I knew was that a new college was being built beside an obscene white concrete road that had obliterated the leafy dark lane, destroying everything in its path. Tillage farms that had supplied the city with vegetables since Adam was a boy disappeared overnight. The Dark Lane, the traditional courting place of Thomas Street Garbos and Marrowbone Lane Valentinos, was going fast. But the real magnitude of what was happening did not hit me until the day I was told that the quarry was being filled in. All the fish would die, and with them a part of me would die too.

Wide-eyed with shock I ran over Dolphin's Barn Bridge and on to the hated concrete road. Soon it came to an end where men were labouring spreading stone, and beyond even more men were digging away the fertile earth. I was in a strange land now that I did not recognize. The trees, the bushes, the few farmhouses were all gone, so I followed the carts that were taking away Dublin's market garden and came to the quarry.

It was true! Before my very eyes the earth poured into the black water on this November day. All around me men were shouting at horses, telling them to "Back up, yeh bastard, stand still", and then there was a crash as another cart tipped up and two or more tons of displacement sent the fish scurrying.

The perch would be well fed this winter, gorged on worms, and there would be huge fish to be caught before all died. For the Corporation were there, too, spewing filth and garbage well back from the dangerous edge. They had two men permanently on site to spread it, whereas the carters had to spread their own. They were being paid by the load, these men who had lived by carrying cabbage, mangolds and turnips to the market. They were making the last wages most of them would ever see, for their life's blood was pouring into the insatiable quarry, and house foundations by the hundred were turning the green fields into a local Flanders.

If the carters felt any of this they gave no sign. They were a proud breed, "horsey men" who were following their fathers before them. There was always a day's work for a horse and cart, and the owner tipped his cap to no man; he punched no factory time-clock, nor ever would. They were small, tough, Liberties men mostly, like Jem Smith, whose son sat in the same classroom as me and whom I now saw backing up a fine deep-chested working cob, the pride of his heart, towards the quarry. The cart had been freshly painted, the leather harness shone, the horse brasses gleamed on the golden chest of the four-year-old.

There was no shouting from Jem as he backed her up slowly and with loving care, but suddenly all hell broke loose as the soil, eroded at its base by the vengeful quarry, slid from under the horse's hooves. She was screaming and squealing, smelling death; Jem wide-eyed, panting, sobbing, trying to hold her and prepared to go with her rather than give in. In my short life the quarry had claimed seven victims and now, with a last dying kick, was going to kill a fine horse and, for good measure, its owner. Only the other men, who by main force held him back, saved him. The horse and cart hit the water with a tremendous splash and in a second had disappeared. All that was left was fleeing waves, and the original bank was back, with twenty feet out a rising column of bubbles. And, of course, poor Jem, who now cast the whip after all the rest.

He made no sound, just stood there as his whole existence crumbled away. He could never again aspire to a horse and cart, and anyway the day of the horse was done. . . and so was Jem. I was looking at half a man now, broken on the wheel of life, never again to be whole. I saw him many times after, always drunk, somehow managing to get the price of a bottle of red Biddy, reeling through Dolphin's Barn, always cursing the quarry. I never went near the place again.

It is now Sundrive Road Park, a pleasant open space, but every time I drive past it I see in my mind's eye a rotting cart and a skeleton horse, seventy feet below. And a man who would have been better off with them. I go quickly past.

BRANDON

Man of The Triple Name
John B. Keane

'There is a wild animal after descending from the mountains and it is the man of the triple name, Dan Paddy Andy.'

With these words and many more Archdeacon Browne denounced the last of the great Irish matchmakers, whose 'ballrooms of romance' offered relief from grinding poverty and suffocating religiosity. Dan Paddy Andy's character and times, his wit and escapades, are magnificently described by John B. Keane.

'Hugely enjoyable.' *In Dublin.*

'Anybody who enjoys old-style storytelling at its best should reach for *Man of the Triple Name.*' *Irish Post.*

'Hilarious social history.' *Boston Irish News.*

'This lyrical, most human and highly humorous book.' *The Irish Times.*

The Bodhrán Makers:
John B. Keane

A novel of conflict and feeling; a story of people driven to rebel.

'John B. Keane's best yarn yet.' *Belfast Telegraph.*

'The book has everything. . . John B. Keane can paint real life pictures of rural life just as Thomas Hardy captured English rural life.' *Andersonstown News.*

'An important and valuable book.' *Irish Press.*

'Told with a vigour and vivacity which keeps the attention riveted.' *The Irish Times.*

'The themes of emigration and repression and the Irish natural sense of rebellion are as relevant today as they were in the 1950s.' *Evening Press.*

Show Us The Moon

Lar Redmond

Show Us The Moon offers a rich portrait of the essential Dublin and of the wit and vitality of Dublin people.

Lar Redmond, author of *Emerald Square*, writes and speaks with the authentic voice of the Liberties of Dublin where he grew up in the 1920s and 30s. His colourful, vibrant stories convey the humour and resilience of Dubliners in the face of poverty and hardship.

Of his previous book reviewers have written:
'There is a teeming sense of life and activity, and Mr Redmond is no slouch at telling a good tale well.' *Sunday Press*.
'A great read, honest and well written. . . So, dear readers, into the bin with the epic sagas. . . for this book is ideal.' *Evening Herald*.

The Heart of the City

Ronan Sheehan & Brendan Walsh

The heart of any city is its people, and in this unique book readers will encounter the people of the so-called 'inner city', people who belong to the oldest working class communities in the country.

This is no evocation of 'the rare oul' times', nor is it a study of architectural or literary heritage; neither is it a sociological study of a 'problem area'. Instead it is a portrait in words and pictures of the lives of the people who have most of all had to live with the consequences of the destruction of Dublin.

No Time For Love

Hugo Meenan

A novel of guerrilla warfare from a former member of both the British Army and the IRA.

'It's the best novel of its kind that I've ever read, because it's the only one. It's written from deep inside.' Eamonn McCann, *Hot Press*.

'An exciting thriller – action packed and very imaginative.' *Socialist Worker*.

'An easy but rewarding read.' *Andersonstown News*.

'His writing is not polished but it does have a capacity for stark description and his knowledge of weaponry and guerilla tactics show evidence of his experience.' *Southern Star*.

Schnitzer O'Shea

Donall Mac Amhlaigh

'This delightful novel is a satire on poets and their adopted lifestyles, on Irish intellectuals and perhaps on English landladies. . . Mr Mac Amhlaigh is an excellent master of English prose.' *Daily Telegraph*.

'I enjoyed the book's joyous air of leg pulling immensely and, for anyone who wants cheering up, I would recommend it unreservedly.' *Sunday Press*.

'A great read, packed with wit.' *Cork Examiner*.

'Highly amusing and absorbing.' *Irish Independent*.

'A chuckle per page.' *Irish Post*.

'It's that rare thing: an excellent comic novel.' *Evening Herald*.